TRUDE MOSTUE

WILD ABOUT ANIMALS

a book of beastly behaviour

MADCAP

Acknowledgements

The author would like to thank everyone at Longleat Safari Park
for their help during the photo shoot for this book.

Picture Credits

André Deutsch would like to thank the following for providing photographs and for permission
to reproduce copyright material. While every effort has been made to trace and acknowledge
all copyright holders, we would like to apologise for any errors or ommissions.

Associated Press page 110, **David Boag** pages 26, 29, 33, 48, 50, 51, 71, 84b, & 105; **Bristol Evening Post** page 4;
Bruce Coleman Collection pages 5 (Jeff Goodman), 8, 12 & 13 (John Cancalosi), 14, 15 (John Cancalosi), 16 (Werner Layer),
17 (John Cancalosi), 31 (Dr MP Kahl), 35 both (Jorg & Petra Wegner), 36 (Hans Reinhard), 37 (Jane Burton), 41 & 42 (Pacific Stock),
43 (Jeff Foott), 43 (Franco Banfi), 49 (Steven C. Kaufman), 56 (Rod Williams), 57 (Michael Freeman), 58 (Jorg & Petra Wegner),
59 (Peter Davey), 60 (Animal Ark), 61 (Leonard Lee Rue), 62 (Werner Layer), 63 & 65t (Jan & Des Bartlett), 65b (Alain Compost),
74 (Joe McDonald), 75 (Dennis Green), 76 (MPL Fogden), 78 (Stephen Krasemann), 79t (Jeff Foott), 79b (Mark Carwardine), 80t (Johnny Johnson),
84t (Hans Reinhard), 87t (Gunter Ziesler), 96 (Staffan Widstrand), 97 (MPL Fogden), 98 (Staffan Widstrand), 99 (MPL Fogden), 102 (Staffan Widstrand),
104 (Jorg & Petra Wegner), 106t (Allan G Potts), 106b (Gordon Langsbury) & 107 (Sir Jeremy Grayson); **Commonwealth Secretariat** page 110;
FLPA pages 88 (Frank W Lane), 90 (John Tinning), 93 (Martin B Wither) & 95 (Frank W Lane); **Don Last** pages 30-31, 32t, 34, 39, 66, 67, 69, 70, 72, 73,
85, 100, 101, 103, 108 & Trude on 110; **Trude Mostue** pages 22, 25 & 68; **NHPA** pages 9 & 10 (ANT), 11 (Don Watts), 18 (Nigel J Dennis),
19 (Anthony Bannister), 20 (Nigel J Dennis), 21 (Anthony Bannister), 27 (Daniel Heuclin), 28 (John Hayward), 52 & 53 (David E Myers),
81 (Daniel Heuclin), 82 (Dr Ivan Polunin), 83 (Waina Cheng Ward), 89 (Joe Blossom), 91 (T Kitchen & V Hurst), 92 (Daniel Heuclin)
& 94 (Anthony Bannister); **Planet Earth Pictures** pages 54 & 55 (Doc White).

Front cover: pictures of Trude Mostue by **Don Last**.
Back cover: pictures of rabbit & hedgehog by **David Boag**; koala by **Bruce Coleman Collection**; elephant shrew by Daniel Heuclin, **NHPA**.

First published in 1999 by Madcap Books,
an imprint of André Deutsch Ltd
76 Dean Street
London W1V 5HA
www.vci.co.uk

Text copyright © Trude Mostue 1999
Scientific Editor: Emily Bethell

ISBN
0-233-99684-2

Design and Editorial
Design/Section, Frome, Somerset

Reprographics by Radstock Reproductions, Midsomer Norton, Bath
Printed and Bound in the UK by Butler & Tanner Limited, Frome and London

Information on conservation status came from:
IUCN Red List of Threatened Animals, Baillie & Groombridge (Eds.), IUCN, Gland, Switzerland, 1996.

Information on life history variables came from:
Grzimek's Encyclopedia of Mammals, S.P. Parker (Ed.),
McGraw-Hill Publishing Company, New York, 1988.

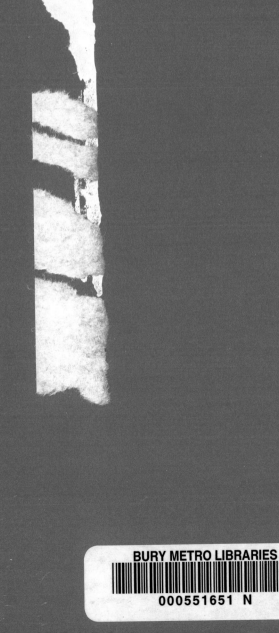

Contents

Introduction 4

Part 1
Monotremes – an order of their own 8

Part 2
Marvellous marsupials 12

Part 3
Placentals x-posed 18

Glosssary 111

i ntroduction

Hi! I'm Trude.

You may recognise
me as the Norwegian
vet from the BBC's
Vets in Practice.

As a vet, or 'animal doctor', I
have treated sick and injured
animals from all over the
world. I have been 'wild about
animals' ever since I was a
young girl and it is a dream
come true to work with them
now that I am a grown-up. At
the moment I am working as
a vet in Somerset and I also
look after the animals at
Longleat Safari Park.

Apart from the incredible
variety of animals there are in
the world, what amazes me
most is how much we can
learn about our pets by
looking at the behaviour of
their wild relatives. I have
written this book to help you
understand why your pets
behave the way they do.

Have you ever wondered
why your dog circles around
its basket before it goes to
sleep? Or why cats dig their
claws into your lap before
they sit down? Or why most
rabbits are called Thumper? Or
why guinea-pigs make such
excellent pets, why hamsters
store food in their cheeks and
gerbils almost never drink?

I have studied and worked
with all kinds of animals and
there are so many it can get
very confusing. To make
things easier for you I have
only included **mammals** in
this book. You may not know
how to identify a **mammal**,
but by the time you have
read this book you will be an
expert. After all, it's easy
when you know how.

What is a mammal?

You and I are **mammals**, but we are not the only ones. Just look around you at the animal world and see if you can recognise any others – maybe even your own pet!

Look at the picture of this gorilla and her baby. It gives you the clues you need to recognise a mammal:

All mammals feed their babies on milk from the mother's mammary glands. Mammals have hair on their body. Mammals have sweat glands, fat for insulation and are warm-blooded.

There are three groups of mammals:

 monotremes – that lay eggs and live in Australia e.g. duck-billed platypus

 marsupials – that have pouches e.g. koalas

 placentals – that give birth to live young e.g. manatees

Some mammals hunt and eat other animals and are called **carnivores**, some eat plants and are called **herbivores**. Some eat insects, and yes, they're called **insectivores**. Others eat both animals and plants – they are called **omnivores**.

Welcome to the world of mammals!

So, now you know what a mammal is, I would like to show you some of the most weird and wonderful mammals I have come across. Some of them you will have heard of, perhaps even have as pets. But others you will not know, and you may be surprised by how much humans have yet to learn about the animal world to which we ourselves belong.

To make it easier for you to find your way around I have divided the book into three main sections, one for each of the different groups of mammal: **monotremes**, **marsupials** and **placentals**. The first two sections are very small. This is because there are very few mammals in these two groups. The third section is longer and you will probably be more familiar with the animals found there, like hamsters, gerbils and guinea-pigs.

There is a **glossary** at the back to help you with words you may not have come across before. All the words that are included in this glossary can be found in **bold** in the main text.

Let's begin our journey

Let me start by introducing you to the mammals in this book. As you now know they are divided into three groups: 1 **monotremes**, 2 **marsupials** and 3 **placentals**. Each group has different mammals in it and the three groups are split into 20 **orders**. Each **order** contains animals which are closely related, for example both rabbits and hares are classed together in the order lagomorpha.

Below is the mammal tree of **orders**. If you'd like to learn more about class, order, family, genus and species, turn to the glossary at the back of the book.

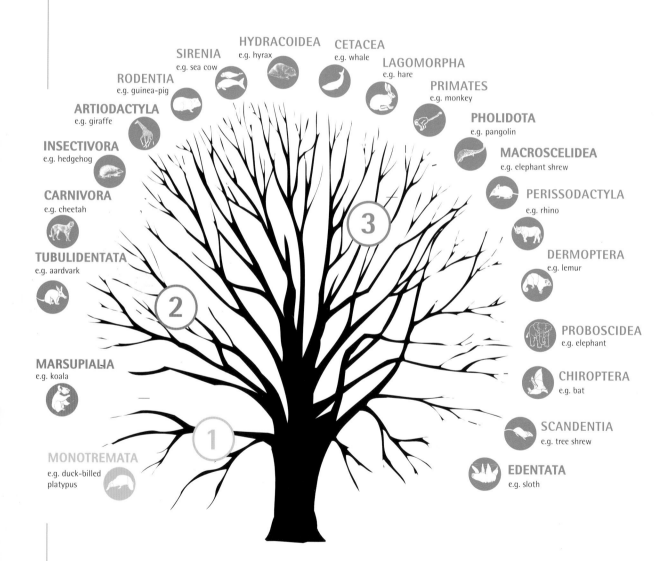

HYDRACOIDEA
e.g. hyrax

CETACEA
e.g. whale

LAGOMORPHA
e.g. hare

SIRENIA
e.g. sea cow

PRIMATES
e.g. monkey

RODENTIA
e.g. guinea-pig

PHOLIDOTA
e.g. pangolin

ARTIODACTYLA
e.g. giraffe

MACROSCELIDEA
e.g. elephant shrew

INSECTIVORA
e.g. hedgehog

PERISSODACTYLA
e.g. rhino

CARNIVORA
e.g. cheetah

3

DERMOPTERA
e.g. lemur

TUBULIDENTATA
e.g. aardvark

2

PROBOSCIDEA
e.g. elephant

CHIROPTERA
e.g. bat

MARSUPIALIA
e.g. koala

SCANDENTIA
e.g. tree shrew

1

MONOTREMATA
e.g. duck-billed platypus

EDENTATA
e.g. sloth

Conservation

You will notice as you read through this book that many of the animals included are now regarded as endangered. This means that they are in danger of becoming extinct.

This can happen for a number of reasons, and unfortunately most of the reasons involve human beings. Too often, humans and animals are competing for space to live in. For too long animals have been over-hunted for their skins or their meat, and humans remain the only animals that hunt for fun.

As the human population of the world increases we need more and more space. This means cutting down trees to build houses, or worse still, cutting down forests to make more space for farms. In many cases, this development results in a loss of habitat for the animals that lived on the land or in the forests. They have nowhere to go and nowhere to get food. Pandas in China and tigers in India are both good examples of this and both are now regarded as endangered.

As a result of this, the conservation of these endangered animals and their habitat is becoming increasingly important. Conservationists are trying to maximise the chances of survival of endangered species. Zoos do this by breeding animals in captivity and then releasing them back into the wild, and National Parks, particularly in Africa, provide a natural environment in which the animals can live and be protected from hunters at the same time. The rhinos of Africa, once close to extinction, now have a good chance of survival because of several zoo breeding programmes throughout the world.

Next time you're at the zoo take a look at the breeding programmes they run and you will see which animals are endangered.

Because of the increasing importance of conservation I have included a Conservation Status report for each animal with a map of where they live and a colour coding to indicate how rare they are in their natural habitat.

CONSERVATION STATUS

- Endangered and likely to become extinct
- Vulnerable to extinction
- Becoming more rare and at some risk
- Common and not in any immediate danger

There is also a 'mystery mammal' on page 109 – see if you can guess what it is from the clues.

Good luck!

duck-billed platypus

CLASS	Mammalia
ORDER	Monotremata
FAMILY	Ornithorhynchidae
GENUS	*Ornithorhynchus*
SPECIES	*anatinus*

In close up

I shall start our journey through the world of mammals with the duck-billed platypus. I know they are comical-looking, but they are also one of the oldest species of mammals.

Platypuses appear to be half reptile half mammal, but if we look more closely we can see the key mammalian features: warm blood, fur and milk produced by glands.

Because it lives in water the duck-billed platypus is called **amphibious**. And because it does most of its hunting at night we call it **nocturnal**.

You can see from the picture below how the duck-billed platypus got its name.

The duck-like bill is covered with leathery, sensitive skin, and the body is covered with a fur coat. This is essential as the waters they live in can get very cold in winter.

Unlike any other **order** of mammals, female monotremes lay soft-shelled eggs. They lay two eggs in a specially dug burrow in the riverbank. Hatchling babies use an egg-tooth to break out of the egg shell, very much like birds do.

Habitat

Like me, the duck-billed platypus just loves to swim, and does this in the rivers of east Australia and Tasmania. The streamlined body, beaver-like tail, short legs and webbed feet make the platypus an excellent swimmer. It 'rows' itself through the water using its feet like paddles, and can move surprisingly fast in pursuit of food.

Below: The duck-billed platypus just loves to swim. Its webbed feet (right) help it swim surprisingly fast.

WILD STATS

PREDATORS	**dingoes** and humans
LENGTH	40-55 cm
WEIGHT	7-22 kg
LIFESPAN	unrecorded in the wild, 17 years in captivity

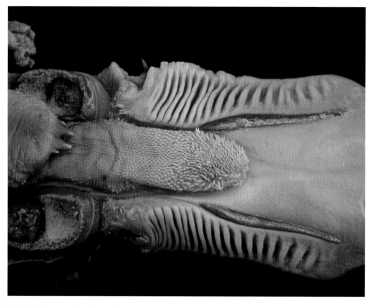

This is the underside of a platypus's bill, and shows its special split tongue .

Diet

The duck-billed platypus is a **carnivore**. It eats snails, insects and other small animals that live in water. To catch its **prey** the platypus swims along the bottom of the river, sweeping its bill from side to side and storing its catch in its cheeks. It then comes to the surface and swallows the food using a very special tongue which is split in two.

CONSERVATION STATUS

Common only in Australia and Tasmania. Also found in New Guinea.

AUSTRALIA

TASMANIA

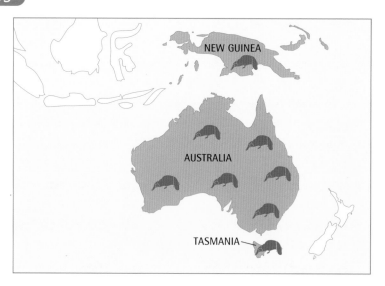

NEW GUINEA

AUSTRALIA

TASMANIA

Social life

Unlike me, the duck-billed platypus is a **solitary** animal. It is also **territorial** and digs caves into the riverbank, patrolling its **territory** along specific patrol routes. Male duck-billed platypuses are masters in chemical warfare. They have a venom spur on their ankle which can be used as a weapon against **predators** and in fights between males during the mating season. The spur can inject enough poison to kill a dog-sized animal and would certainly cause a human a lot of pain.

Left: The platypus is amphibious, and swims along the bottom of rivers in search of insects and other small animals to eat.

FASCINATING FACTS

- The first mention of the duck-billed platypus was made by naturalist George Shaw (1751-1813) in 1799. He called it the 'duck-like flatfoot', but this was later changed to the 'duck-billed platypus' – a funny name all the same.

- Monotremes have only one hole (called the **cloaca**) through which to go to the toilet and lay eggs, just like a reptile. All other mammals have two or three holes. This is why they are known as mono- (one) tremes- (hole). Spiny echidnas are another kind of monotreme.

- The oldest monotreme skeleton is 85 million years old. That makes it the oldest mammal skeleton ever found in Australia.

- When diving for food the platypus closes its eyes, ears and nostrils to stop water and dirt entering them. I have to use goggles, noseplugs and earplugs.

- The duck-billed platypus can locate prey underwater, using its bill which it moves from side to side to detect electrical pulses (in a similar way to sharks).

crazy about koalas

CLASS	Mammalia
ORDER	Marsupialia
FAMILY	Phascolarctidaea
GENUS	*Phascolarctus*
SPECIES	*cinerus*

In close up

The cute and cuddly koala is one of my favourite mammals.

With a woolly coat, baby face, stubby nose and fluffy ears, koalas are like living teddy bears – I just can't help wanting to cuddle them! The feature for which the marsupials are most famous is the pouch. In koalas this pouch is, in true Aussie fashion, upside down!

Male koalas communicate by making a low grunting sound, which reminds me of a pig. The female must raise and carry her young alone so she gives birth to just one at a time. If a baby is accidentally abandoned it will wail loudly, an eerie sound – to me it sounds just like a human baby crying.

Habitat

Koalas, like most marsupials, live in Australia (oppossums are also marsupials and can be found as far away as South America). With their sharp claws and strong grip they are excellent climbers. Because they spend all day in the trees they are known as **arboreal**. They only come down to the ground if they absolutely have to! They can even sleep balanced in the fork of a tree, which is handy since they spend a staggering 18 hours a day snoozing!

Diet

Koalas are **herbivores**. Eucalyptus is their favourite

A wooly-coated, baby-faced, stubby-nosed and fluffy-eared koala bear.

CONSERVATION STATUS

The koala is now
a protected **species**.

AUSTRALIA

AUSTRALIA

*Female koalas with young are often
solitary, staying away from other
koalas until the young are reared and
ready to forage for themselves.*

food, but they are fussy eaters and only eat 20 of the 350 types of eucalyptus found in Australia. Most koalas NEVER drink – they get all the water they need from their food. Mother koalas teach their young which leaves to eat by bending small branches down to the offspring's nose so it gets used to the smell of edible plants. Though they are primarily **nocturnal** creatures, koalas may also occasionally come out to feed during the day.

Social life

Females with young are often **solitary**, while males are more **social** and will protect several females in a **harem**. Males become **territorial** only during the mating season. They mark the trees forming the boundary to their area using special **scent glands** on their chests. They also use loud barks to attract females. The louder the bark and the nicer the smell, the more chance a male has of mating with lots of females.

WILD STATS

PREDATORS	dogs, **dingoes** and humans
LENGTH	82 cm (males), 70 cm (females)
WEIGHT	5-12 kg
LIFESPAN	20 years in the wild

5 FASCINATING FACTS

- The name koala comes from the **Aboriginal** language and literally means 'no drink' because the koala never drinks.

- The scientific name for the koala – *Phascolarctu* – is taken from the Greek words *phaskolon* (pouch) and *arktos* (bear) and the Latin word *cinerus* (ash coloured).

- Koalas have quite a disgusting way of weaning their young. The mother's pouch faces her bottom. Young koalas are unable to go straight from drinking milk to eating eucalyptus, so they must eat processed eucalyptus to get used to it. To do this they feed on the mother's dung as she produces it – yuk!

- 100 years ago Australia had millions of koalas climbing about in its trees. Humans hunting the defenceless animals for sport and the spread of forest fires, which were often started intentionally, have led to a huge decrease in the koala's numbers. Hunting koalas is now illegal.

- An even greater threat arose because of the koala's lovely soft fur coat. Hunters wiped out the animals in many areas of Australia to take the soft fur, which fetched large sums of money in other countries.

The one thing that koalas do really well ... is sleep. In fact, it is common for koalas to sleep for up to 18 hours a day.

kangaroo kickers

CLASS	Mammalia	
ORDER	Marsupialia	
FAMILY	Macropodidae	Potoroidae
GENUS	*Hypsiprimnodon*	*Macropus*
SPECIES	*moschatus* (red kangaroo)	*rufus* (muskrat kangaroo)

In close up

When I think of kangaroos I picture large animals hopping across the grasslands of Australia, and I expect you do too. However, the smallest kangaroo is the size of a rat, lives in the rainforests of northern Australia and is **arboreal**! The largest **terrestrial** kangaroos are the size of humans but have a much deadlier kick. As with their fellow marsupials, the koalas, female kangaroos have the characteristic pouch in which they carry their young. A baby kangaroo is called a 'joey'.

Large, muscular back legs can carry the bigger species at high speed – faster than I can run, anyway. The long muscular tail acts as a 'fifth leg' and gives extra push-off from the ground for hopping. I've often wished I had five hands, but never five legs!

Newborn kangaroos are tiny and naked. The newborn joey must climb, unaided by

The larger species of kangaroo can run much faster than humans.

the mother and guided by smell, from the **cloaca** to the pouch. There, it attaches its mouth to a teat and suckles for several weeks, growing very quickly. Kangaroos only give birth to one joey at a time. The pouch is a comfortable size for one, but as the joey gets bigger you can see why two would be a crowd!

Wallabies are a type of kangaroo, too, but generally smaller and fatter. The nicest wallaby I ever met was Keeley, a small female at Longleat, who was abandoned by her mother and then hand-reared by humans. Because of human contact from that age, she was very relaxed around me and we became friends.

Baby kangaroos, or 'joeys', grow at an alarming rate and rapidly get too big to fit in mum's pouch.

Habitat

Kangaroos and wallabies live in Australia and New Guinea.

There are red kangaroos, savannah-dwelling kangaroos, rock wallabies and tree-climbing, bear-like wallabies. In fact, kangaroos and wallabies come in all shapes and sizes and live in all kinds of unexpected places.

Diet

Smaller species (like the muskrat kangaroo) are **omnivorous**, feeding on fruits, insects, worms and nuts. Larger species (like the red kangaroo) are **herbivorous** and feed on grasses and green plants.

Social life

Kangaroos are **social** and **nocturnal**. Males take part in spectacular wrestling displays to impress and mate with females. When things get really rough they kick each other with powerful hind limbs (a kick from a kangaroo can kill a human – so don't get too close!)

WILD STATS

PREDATORS **dingoes**, pythons and birds often prey on smaller kangaroo species. Humans cull and shoot them for sport and meat

HEIGHT 15.7–27.3 cm (muskrat kangaroos), to 100 cm (red kangaroos)

WEIGHT 3.6–6.8 kg (muskrat kangaroos), to 17–84 kg (red kangaroos)

LIFESPAN unknown for muskrat kangaroos, 20 years (red kangaroos)

- The first marsupials to be discovered by Europeans were oppossums and they came from Brazil in South America. The first Europeans to see kangaroos were Dutch seamen in 1629, although their reports were not confirmed until 1770, when Captain James Cook rediscovered them.

- If a female kangaroo becomes pregnant while she has too many young to look after she can delay the birth of the next joey until a more convenient time – if only humans could do that.

- Sometimes even quite large young kangaroos return to their mother's pouch to hide in times of danger. It's very funny to watch a joey dive headfirst into a

pouch which is a bit too small, leaving its flailing legs sticking out.

- Kangaroos have a stomach which is divided into several parts. This means they can **regurgitate** food and eat it again, just like cows do.

- In the nineteenth century, red-necked wallabies were released into the wild in England, but they have long since been wiped out by hunters. However, there is a small population of red-necked wallabies living in the Peak District and on an island in Loch Lomond!

This sweet little thing is a rock wallaby. Rock wallabies are now regarded as a threatened species due to loss of habitat.

CONSERVATION STATUS

Most kangaroo species are common. Some tree-dwelling species are threatened by the destruction of their forest habitat.

NEW GUINEA

AUSTRALIA

- - - Areas of Grassland

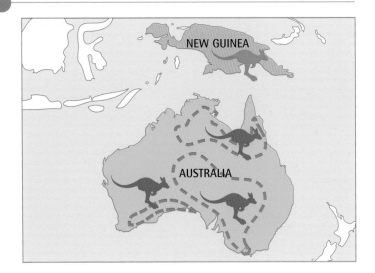

NEW GUINEA

AUSTRALIA

adventures with aardvarks

CLASS	Mammalia
ORDER	Tubulidentata
FAMILY	Orcyteropodidae
GENUS	*Oryctopus*
SPECIES	*afer* (African aardvark)

In close up

Aardvarks are funny looking creatures. Look at the pictures and you will see they have a stocky body, arched back, short legs, long spoon-shaped claws, greyish-pinkish skin with little hair, a long tapering head and long tube-like ears. They walk on tiptoes and I think the end of their nose looks like a pig's snout.

You may be surprised to know that aardvarks look so weird because of the ants and termites they feed on. As strange as it may sound, feeding on ants means that aardvark noses and tongues have grown very long to probe deep into termite mounds and to pick up lots of squirming ants in one swoop. Of course, it makes things a lot easier to break down the termite mounds first. So aardvarks also have strong front digging legs and long claws for this.

There is another ant-eating mammal in this book called a pangolin. Can you spot the similarities between the two; do you think they look like each other because they both eat the same food?

Because they spend all their time on the ground (where their insect **prey** lives) they are **terrestrial**. One time, when I was in Africa, I was

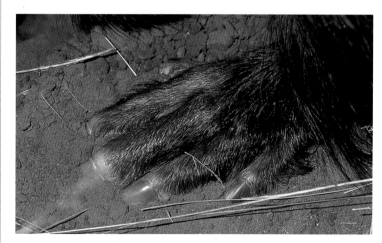

Strong claws make short work of termite mounds – an aardvark's favourite meal.

WILD STATS

PREDATORS	humans, lions, leopards and hyenas. Pythons may occasionally enter burrows and take young aardvarks
LENGTH	110 cm
HEIGHT	60 cm
WEIGHT	60–80 kg
LIFESPAN	23 years in captivity

An aardvark, with its long snout and big ears cannot be confused with any other mammal.

watching an aardvark running around looking for termites. Aardvarks must have very poor eyesight because it was bumping into everything!

Habitat

Aardvarks live in sub-Saharan Africa. They spend the day underground in long, zig-zagging tunnels which they dig themselves. Because they are active at night aardvarks are **nocturnal**. Aardvarks live on **savannahs**, plains and in rainforests (or anywhere with a good supply of termites). When digging their tunnels they fold their ears back and close their nostrils to keep out dirt, ants and **termites**.

Diet

Aardvarks are **insectivores**, feeding mainly on ants and **termites**. As with anteaters and pangolins, this diet means they have a long snout and a long, worm-like sticky tongue. Aardvarks get their water from gourds, which are vegetables known locally as 'aardvark cucumbers'. In order to find termite mounds aardvarks need a good sense of smell

5 FASCINATING FACTS

- The aardvark is also known as the 'antbear' because it eats ants and **termites** and looks like a bear.

- While aardvarks look like anteaters and pangolins they are, in fact, more closely related to hoofed mammals like horses.

- Aardvarks are amazingly fast diggers. If threatened with danger the aardvark can dig a shallow burrow and hide in seconds.

- Aardvarks have a funny way of moving around. When an aardvark comes out of its burrow it will stay motionless for up to 10 minutes, sniffing the air for any sign of danger before sprinting off, pausing again to sniff the air, sitting up, raising its ears and turning its head in every direction. It then makes a few jumps and bounds away in search of food.

- When frightened, an aardvarks make a bleating sound, just like a sheep.

Once it has got into the ant or termite nest, the aardvark uses its long sticky tongue to eat the insects, their eggs and larvae.

Although not common, aardvarks are not thought to be endangered.

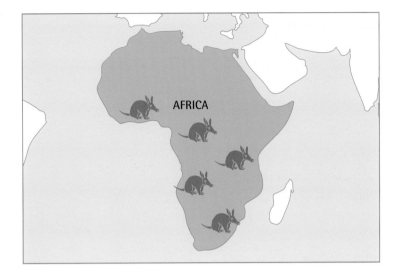

AFRICA

and if you watch an aardvark closely you will see it is always sniffing in search of food.

Social life

Aardvarks are **solitary**, spending most of their time alone, although sometimes they defend a **territory** in pairs. Females give birth to one young at a time. Young aardvarks stay with the mother for the first six months and then dig their own burrow nearby. The young will continue to search for **termites** with the mother. The female offspring will continue to live nearby, but the males will eventually move away.

Not such a good view this time, for us that is! The aardvark here has got into a termite mound and is munching happily on its supper.

chasing cheetahs

CLASS	Mammalia
ORDER	Carnivora
FAMILY	Felidae
GENUS	*Acinonyx*
SPECIES	*jubatus*

In close up

If you asked me which was my favourite mammal then I would have to say the cheetah. Their head and body are streamlined to help them run faster and their legs are long, thin, light and incredibly powerful. The spine is a flexible rod that acts like a spring, allowing the back legs to push harder and the front legs to extend further. The hard, sharp toe pads on the soles of their feet are even designed to act as brakes so they can stop or turn suddenly. But I think the most striking features are their eyes. They have the most beautiful eye markings.

I met two tame cheetahs when I was in Botswana, in Africa. To my surprise, they were as affectionate as my kitten at home, nudging and brushing up against me and purring loudly. Despite the

This is one of my favourite cheetahs in the world. She was like a purring machine and just as friendly as my pet kitten.

image people have of them as killing machines these cheetahs were safe to be near because I am larger than the animals they normally hunt. However, whatever size you are, I wouldn't recommend getting too near.

If you look at a domestic cat's claws you will notice they can retract them (pull them in), but these wild cats have claws that are more like a dog's than a cat's. Cheetahs

cannot retract their claws, for one good reason: claws that grip the ground when they run help them to move even faster. Their claws are kept blunt because their paws do not have the protective sheath of skin that most other cats have.

If I lived in Africa and had enough space I would run a sanctuary for orphaned cheetahs similar to one I know of in Namibia.

Habitat

Cheetahs live on the African savannah and grasslands. Because they are **diurnal** their fur is a golden colour which keeps them camouflaged when stalking **prey**. Roaming these open areas to hunt has led to their unique and beautiful physical features, but because they are so specialised they cannot adapt easily to new environments. As their habitat is increasingly in demand for human development these beautiful cats come ever closer to the point of extinction.

Cheetahs normally give birth to twin cubs, and aren't they just the most lovely fluffy balls of fun?

Built for speed, cheetahs can reach speeds of up to 70 kph when in sight of their supper.

Diet

Cheetahs are **carnivores**. Their favourite **prey** are small to medium sized antelopes. But small groups of males may kill larger **prey** like zebra and wildebeest. They are excellent at catching these animals (with a 50 per cent success rate they are one of the most successful feline hunters). But cheetahs are shy animals and lose many of their hard-won kills to more ferocious lions, hyenas, wild dogs and even vultures. They don't just lose their catch because they are shy, either. The average cheetah is so exhausted after pursuing its **prey** that it has to rest for 20-30 minutes before it can eat. This gives scavengers plenty of time to move in and move off with the cheetah's dinner.

Social life

Cheetahs are **solitary** and like to spend their time alone. The greatest number of cheetahs I know of that have been seen together in the wild is three. These were males who sometimes form small groups known as 'coalitions'. Cheetahs usually give birth to twins, known as cubs. The cubs are incredibly cute fluffy balls of fun. They are born with a thick coat of long grey fur with no spots which is shed when they are three months old, when the new solid-spot fur will grow.

5 FASCINATING FACTS

- The cheetah is the fastest mammal in the world. But while they may be excellent sprinters they are not so good at long distance running. In fact cheetahs have been caught by humans chasing them on foot as over long distances they are easy to catch up with.

- Cheetahs purr – like your cat – but it is so loud it sounds like a car engine.

- The markings on each cheetah's tail are unique and can be used to identify individuals – just like fingerprints.

- Without using the muscular tail as a stabiliser cheetahs would not be able to change direction so easily at top speed.

- Because cheetahs are such brilliant hunters and can be easily tamed,` the Rajahs of India used to train cheetahs to hunt for them.

Cheetahs have a distinctive tear-mark running from the eye to the mouth.

CONSERVATION STATUS

AFRICA

There are only about 10,000 cheetahs left in the wild. They are hunted by man for their skins, but their numbers are also declining because of loss of habitat, high infant death rates, often to other large predators like lions, and high death rates among fighting males.

AFRICA

hairy hedgehogs

CLASS	Mammalia
ORDER	Insectivora
FAMILY	Erinaceidae
GENUS	6 genera including: *Erinaceus* *Hemiechinus*
SPECIES	16 species including: *europaeus* *auritus* (European hedgehog) (moonrat)

In close up

Now here is a wild animal you can find in your back garden. The best time to see hedgehogs is at night during the spring when they are particularly active. At that time of year the warm weather wakes them up from their winter **hibernation**. As you can imagine, after several months of not eating they are incredibly hungry and may just pass through your garden in search of some tasty morsels of food.

As a vet I get to see inside the rolled-up hedgehogs that are brought into my surgery. They have a special muscle along their back which allows them to roll up into a ball. Try curling up as tight as a hedgehog. It would be a lot easier if you, too, had this special muscle. Hedgehogs sleep rolled up like this in a

Watch out for hedgehogs in your garden – especially in the spring.

Hedgehogs are born bald, deaf and blind – not a pretty sight.

nest of leaves and will also curl up when frightened.

We are all familiar with spiny hedgehogs, but did you know that moonrats are hedgehogs as well? They don't have spines; in fact they are soft and furry, and look just like hedgehogs who have lost all their spines. Moonrats are the largest insectivores in the world.

Can you spot some of the hedgehog's characteristics in the picture on the left? They all have a large head, pointed snout, wet nose, small eyes and ears, a short tail and sharp claws. True hedgehogs have spines. Moonrats have hair.

Hedgehogs' spines act as defence against being eaten by bigger animals. How many predators would want a mouthful of hedgehog spines? Poor eyesight means hedgehogs have to rely on smell. This is why they spend so much time sniffing the ground as they scuttle along. In fact, baby hedgehogs are born blind. They are also deaf and have soft white spines so are completely dependent on the mother for protection.

Another thing I have noticed from looking closely at hedgehogs in the surgery is that they are breeding grounds for all kinds of biting, stinging and blood-sucking pests like fleas, lice and ticks. Hedgehogs cannot scratch themselves because their arms and legs are too short – they might also spike themselves. To try and combat the pests hedgehogs spit on their spines, but it doesn't look like it makes much of a difference.

Habitat

Hedgehogs are mainly **terrestrial**. They are **territorial** and **nocturnal**. Most hedge-hogs live in the same nest for several years. However, in Asia, Europe and Africa there are some tree species which are more **arboreal**. Moonrats are **nocturnal** and spend the day in tree and rock hollows or under tree roots.

Diet

While they are **insectivores**, and mainly eat insects, hedge-hogs can also eat vegetables, fruit and plants. Some prey on vipers by biting the snake's neck and breaking its back. They are resistant to viper venom which is just as well because a bite from one of these snakes should be lethal for such a small mammal.

Social life

Hedgehogs are **solitary** and are particularly common in small towns, around rubbish dumps and in gardens where they know there will be lots of food. I was surprised the first time I heard a hedgehog make a noise. I expected to hear it squeak like a mouse. Instead, it made puffing sounds which got louder and

WILD STATS

PREDATORS	owls and humans
LENGTH	15–30 cm
WEIGHT	220–1100 g
LIFESPAN	7–8 years (in captivity)

more frequent the more excited it became.

Hedgehogs are the only **insectivores** that are true **hibernators**. This means they sleep all through the winter, living off fat reserves in the body. Their body temperature falls to just 1°C above air temperature and their heart beats very slowly. You or I would die if our bodies became this cold.

Moonrats are constantly alert and sniffing for food and danger as they move along the ground. When it senses a predator a moonrat will dash for a hole or the

When threatened, a hedgehog rolls up and pretends it's a spiky ball. Well, would you pick one up?

CONSERVATION STATUS

Common in Europe, although being forced to adapt to spreading urban environments. Endangered in Asia where logging is severely reducing the numbers of their insect **prey**.

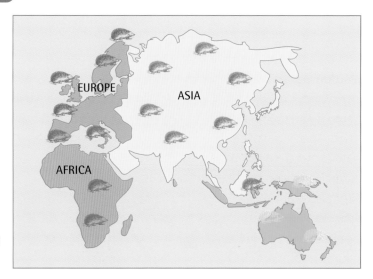

A hedgehog is its own worst enemy – it just loves crossing the road! Ouch!

nearest stream where it submerges itself to hide. They swim with the chin and nose sticking out of the water.

They can even close their nostrils when they dive. Moonrats secrete a foul-smelling substance from their

anal **glands** which smells like garlic. This marks their territory and is so smelly that it can also repel predators.

 FASCINATING FACTS

- Hedgehogs have mouths and stomachs of steel. They can eat poisonous insects that other insectivores avoid and they also eat stinging wasps and bees with no trouble at all. They are even resistant to poisons that kill humans – like arsenic.

- Moonrats are slaves to their tummies. In Malaysia local people catch them in traps baited with bananas, their favourite fruit.

- Because they snuffle about the ground moonrats are sometimes known as 'earth pigs'.

- Hedgehogs love crossing roads and more hedgehogs are killed by getting run over than any other European mammal.

- Hedgehogs can have as many as 10,000 spines. I wonder who counted them all?

giraffes: a tall story

CLASS	Mammalia
ORDER	Artiodactyla
FAMILY	Giraffidae
GENUS	*Giraffa*
SPECIES	*camelopardalis*

In close up

I think of giraffes as the supermodels of the animal world. They have the same number of neck bones as you and I. How come the giraffe has such a long neck? You may well ask. Well, the answer is simple: a giraffe's neck bones are *very* long.

When I was in Botswana, in Africa, I had to dart several giraffes so we could transfer them to a safer area. Because giraffes have such long powerful legs and hard hooves (strong enough to kill a lion) it is dangerous to get too close, so we had to dart them from a helicopter. As we flew towards the herd they looked like dinosaurs striding across the horizon. Once darted we could get near the **sedated** giraffe. The eyelashes were the longest I have seen on any animal and different giraffes had between two and five rounded horns covered in skin. At Longleat I can get close to the giraffes because they have been reared by humans. This makes treating them much easier.

Above left: Both sexes of giraffe carry at least one pair of short bony horns.

Right: The hand-reared giraffes at Longleat are tame and easy to handle.

Although a giraffe's long legs are handy for reaching tasty treetop leaves, they're not so useful when bending down to drink from a waterhole.

Young giraffes are wobbly on their legs to begin with. Imagine trying to walk on stilts – this should give you some idea what it feels like to be a newborn giraffe learning to walk.

What always puzzled me was whether or not giraffes lay down to sleep like we do. With such long legs lying down and standing up must be difficult. In fact, because they are so vulnerable to predators when lying down, they only sleep for two minutes at a time. Some individuals may only get five minutes sleep in a night – that's even less than me when I'm on call at the surgery!

Habitat

Giraffes live in the bush and savannahs of sub-Saharan Africa. While their markings and height make them unmistakable on the open savannah, among trees their spotted markings resemble the bark of the tree trunks – clever! The spotted pattern over their body is different in each animal, so you can use them to identify individuals, rather like our fingerprints.

Diet

Giraffes are **herbivores**. They eat leaves and fresh shoots and especially like acacia leaves. The long legs and *very* long neck mean giraffes can reach the leaves at the tops of trees that other animals cannot reach and it's amazing how long (and blue!) a giraffe's tongue is – few leaves are safely out of reach of this creature. However, as you can see from the picture above, bending down to drink is far more difficult. Again, a long tongue helps lap up water from waterholes.

This is Frank, who was born at Longleat, and is my favourite all-time giraffe. As you can see, he likes me too.

Social life

Giraffes are **social** animals and spend their time in small herds. I once saw a herd of over 50. They are **diurnal**, but are sometimes active on bright nights. Because they must roam over such large distances in search of food giraffes are not **territorial**.

I once saw two giraffes fighting. It was an amazing sight, because giraffes are generally peaceful animals. The two males stood facing one another, reared up their heads and then struck each other on the body and limbs with their necks. Each blow made a loud thud. Eventually, one of them surrendered. To make friends again they rubbed necks gently against each other and then continued to graze side by side. If only humans could be so quick to forgive and forget!

5 —FASCINATING FACTS—

- Giraffes are the tallest mammals in the world!

- Giraffes can jump over a six-foot fence (or a tall human).

- Giraffe tongues are among the longest in the animal kingdom, measuring half a metre!

- Giraffes may be easy to spot, but they will certainly see you first because they have excellent eyesight, not to mention a high viewing post.

- Giraffe's heads are so high above the ground they need special valves in their necks which help blood to reach the brain. The blood vessels also expand and contract to maintain the blood pressure.

As you can see from the photos, giraffes are easy to spot in the open. I have often noticed that savannah-dwelling animals live alongside other species – and this applies to giraffes, too.

This means more eyes to look out for predators and, because they eat different foods, there are no fights over who gets dinner.

A fully-grown giraffe can run at 60 kph.

WILD STATS

PREDATORS young giraffes may be preyed upon by lions, hyenas, leopards, and African wild dogs. To protect the young the herd will surround them. Imagine trying to get through all those powerful kicking legs to reach your **prey** and you will see why this is such an effective means of protection

HEIGHT 1.5–3.3 metres (at the shoulder). Male giraffes may measure up to six metres in height (that's the equivalent of four adult humans standing on each other's shoulders!)

WEIGHT 210–1900 kg

LIFESPAN 25 years in the wild, over 30 years in captivity

CONSERVATION STATUS

AFRICA

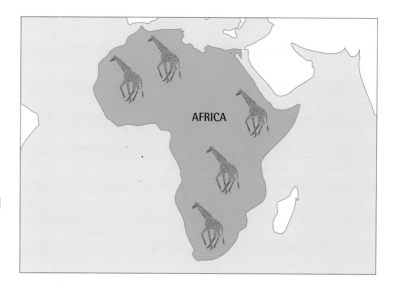

AFRICA

Protected **species**. The greatest threats facing the giraffe are poachers who kill these beautiful animals for their skin. Loss of habitat is also a serious problem.

risking it with rodents

CLASS	Mammalia
ORDER	Rodentia
FAMILY	36 families
GENUS	400 genera: including *Mesocricetus* *Cavia* *Gerbillurus*
SPECIES	1700 species: including *auratus* (golden hamster) *aperea* (guinea-pig) 3 species (gerbil)

In close up

Welcome to my pets' corner. There are so many different rodent **species** I hardly know where to start. So I thought I would talk about those I have had the most experience with, and I suspect you have come across them too: gerbils, hamsters and guinea-pigs. I see these animals every day in my surgery because they are such popular pets. However, while they look similar you may be surprised to learn that there are some very important differences.

Gerbils are similar to hamsters, but if you look closely you will see that they are smaller, have rounder bodies, larger eyes, a hairy tuft at the end of the tail and powerful thighs with long

There are lots of different kinds of guinea-pig, but they're all cute and fluffy and make great pets.

back feet. They are brilliant jumpers. One time a gerbil jumped off the operating table in my surgery and survived – that's the equivalent of a human jumping off a skyscraper!

Guinea-pigs make excellent pets because they are fairly small, eat very little, don't need constant attention and do not smell too much (as long as you clean their cage frequently). There are lots of different kinds, from short- to long-haired, **albino** to black and with all kinds of mixtures in between.

Hamsters don't make the best pets. In fact, they are one of the most dangerous animals I have in my surgery because they have such a ferocious bite. Hamsters spend a lot of

CONSERVATION STATUS

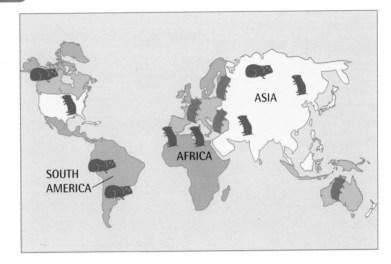

(gerbils)
- Because they are so small and live in uninhabitable places like the desert, gerbils are not under threat from extinction.

(hamsters)
- In the wild, golden hamsters are close to extinction due to the loss of their habitat.

(guinea-pigs)
- Because they live near human settlements, wild cavies are at risk from few predators other than man.

Above and below: Guinea-pigs come in all shapes and sizes, including striped, long-haired, black, white, orange and albino.

time cleaning themselves. Since they are **solitary** (unlike the **social** guinea-pigs) you need to make a big effort to keep their surroundings stimulating. However, they are incredibly cute and if you follow my pointers on pages 38-39 you will have a healthy and happy hamster.

WILD STATS

PREDATORS predatory birds such as owls and eagles

LENGTH 8–13 cm (gerbils), 13–18 cm (hamsters), 25 cm (guinea-pigs)

WEIGHT 15–37 g (gerbils), 100–120 g (hamsters), 600 g–1000 g (guinea-pigs)

LIFESPAN 2–3 years (gerbils), 3 years (hamsters), 5–10 years (guinea-pigs)

Habitat

Wild gerbils live in the deserts and dry areas of Africa and Asia. They are pale in colour so they blend in with the sand and have strong thighs to hop away from predators. During the day they hide in the safety of underground burrows.

Hamsters are energetic and like to run around and dig burrows. These burrows look cosy – they dig bed chambers, food stores and even toilet chambers! In the wild they can be found in south-east Europe and the Near East.

Wild guinea-pigs (who are also called 'cavies') live in South America where they run free, living off scraps of food around human settlements.

Diet

I love watching rodents eat, they look so funny. Because wild gerbils live in the desert, where food is scarce, they have learnt to survive by eating and drinking very little. This makes them easy to look after. To keep water in the body, gerbil pee is concentrated and smells quite pungent. Hamsters have cheek pouches which can be stuffed full of food until they stick out as far as they will go. This portable larder can then be carried to the burrow to be eaten at leisure. They particularly enjoy eating seeds and plant parts, but they are **omnivorous** and also eat earthworms, insects and snails. Guinea-pigs can be fed on grass, hay, leaves, carrots, lettuce, apples, bark, oats and corn. Many of these you will have as leftovers from your own meals, so that makes it cheap as well.

Generally solitary animals, these gerbils pose for a group picture.

Social life

Gerbils and hamsters are both **nocturnal** and **solitary**, which means they don't like being disturbed during the day and are most active during the night.

Guinea-pigs are **social** creatures. By looking at the behaviour of wild guinea-pigs we can learn a lot about pet guinea-pigs. In the wild, guinea-pigs live in colonies where each animal has a rank. Dominant males strut around purring loudly and this has a calming effect on all the others. Females get on better with each other than males, who tend to fight a lot.

If you have pet guinea-pigs you may be lucky enough to watch one giving birth. Their young are born in a quiet corner and the other animals in the group often gather round to watch. They are born with full fur, open eyes, and can even groom themselves straight after birth. The thing I really love about guinea-pigs, as with most animals, is that you get to know their personalities. If you take some time to get to know what your pet likes and dislikes you can make their life more fun.

A hamster, ready to enjoy a big meal.

5 FASCINATING FACTS

- Rodents are the ultimate surviving machines. They live in, on and under the ground in every country in the world (except Antarctica and New Zealand), can run, jump, swim, climb, dig and glide through the air and they eat plants, insects and meat – phew! And if that isn't enough the **order** of rodents has more species than any other mammal **order** in the world.

- All rodents have special 'chisel' teeth that never stop growing. In fact, even fossil rodents from over 57 million years ago have these same teeth.

- Most hamsters which are kept in laboratories and as pets come from a single female and its young. They were dug up in Syria and bred to produce the majority of all hamsters used in labs and kept as pets today.

- While most other hamsters have just four teats the golden hamster has between six and eleven.

- Guinea-pigs were first brought to Britain by the Romans as a source of food. They used to run wild about the British countryside, but now you will only see them as pets.

caring for your pet rodent

Lots of people have rodents as pets, and while they are generally easy to look after, it's worth knowing what they like and what they don't like. After all, a happy pet is much more healthy than an unhappy one.

Gerbils

• Gerbils love burrowing, like hamsters and rabbits. Give your gerbil something to burrow into and hide under (like earth, shredded paper and toilet rolls), but not sand because this will make its nose very sore. You can have lots of fun decorating your pet's cage and your pet will appreciate it too.

• Like hamsters, gerbils are solitary and territorial and so should be kept alone.

• In the wild gerbils feed on grass, seeds and even some insects. Because rodent teeth grow continuously it is important to give your pet a varied diet. Natural items like branches and twigs are good objects to add to the cage for your pet to chew on.

• Gerbils have very big thighs and can jump very high. Make sure there is enough room in the cage for your gerbil to jump around if it wants to.

Hamsters

• Hamsters are active animals that like to search for their food. Try spreading their food around the cage in small parcels so your pet can forage around and build up a store to feed from over the rest of the day.

• Hamsters are solitary animals, so they should be kept alone in the cage. Because of the lack of playmates it is even more important to give them other things to do. How about putting in some ladders for it to climb up and down and tubes it can run through and explore?

• Hamsters often get too fat because they are fed too much. This means they end up dragging their fat tummies on the floor, which can lead to painful infections on the underbelly and genitals.

• I once had a visit from an upset pet-owner who thought his hamster was dead. The poor hamster wasn't dead at all, it had just gone into hibernation for the winter and was in a deep sleep! So don't be surprised when your hamster does the same thing.

• Hamsters are nocturnal. This is why they are often so grumpy when they are picked up in the middle of the day. How would you feel if someone plucked you out of your bed in the middle of the night?

Guinea-pigs

- If you want to keep lots of small rodents together then guinea-pigs are a good choice of pet. However, they do not mix well with other animals. I see lots of guinea-pigs which have been kept with rabbits in the same cage. This is not a good idea because guinea-pigs need to be fed extra vitamin C (in special guinea-pig food) and will become stressed if kept in a cage with rabbits.

- Guinea-pigs love running around, just like rabbits do. Let them run around the garden, but make sure they are protected from cats.

- Guinea-pigs get stressed easily. It is important to house them in a run that has lots of private corners where they can hide. I see many pet guinea-pigs that have died from heart-attacks – they literally die of fright. This is usually because their cage is too small or they have been handled too much. The best way to prevent this is to make sure you handle your pet from a very early age.

Chinchillas are less common but also make good pets.

This will get them used to you and will cause less stress in later life.

- Guinea-pigs eat all the time; that is why they have such big bottoms. If your pet guinea-pig stops eating altogether you should take it to the vet straight away or it will die very quickly. I see a lot of guinea-pigs that this has happened to and it is usually because of a problem with the teeth or stomach. A vet like myself can soon put everything right again.

how now, sea cow?

CLASS Mammalia

ORDER Sirenia

FAMILY Trichechidae

GENUS *Trichechus*

SPECIES 3 species: *manatus* (West Indian manatee), *nunguis,* (Amazonian manatee), *senegalensis* (West African manatee)

In close up

As the name suggests, sea cows, which are also called manatees and dugongs, live in the sea, but they are not really cows. In fact, these odd-looking mammals are more closely related to elephants than cows. Because they live in the sea we call them **aquatic**. To help them swim faster sea cows have a cylindrical (streamlined) body, round tail and front limbs which have transformed into powerful flippers. To help them stay warm they have thick skin and small ears. They also have nails on their 'hands', a muscular lip, and continually growing teeth which are frequently replaced.

Although they spend most of their time underwater manatees must come to the surface to breathe. As they near the surface many manatees are accidentally and fatally injured by boat propellers. Many more survive their injuries but are scarred for life.

So rare are these animals that I have never actually seen one, either in captivity or in the wild. Being so large and having very few predators, manatees are gentle, peace-loving mammals who seldom fight and like to swim around on their own, eating and resting as much as possible.

Habitat

Manatees live in the coastal waters and rivers of Central America. Because they are only found in this part of the world few people have actually seen a wild manatee.

Diet

Sea cows are **herbivores**. Because they live underwater, they feed on plants that grow in rivers and on coastlines. Many such plants are thick and chewy and wear down the manatees' teeth. This is why manatees' teeth never stop growing and are continuously replaced.

Right: The greatest threat to the survival of these gentle giants comes from human development of their natural habitat.

WILD STATS

PREDATORS manatees' only predators are humans who hunt them for meat

LENGTH 2.5-4.5 metres (including tail)

WEIGHT 200-600 kg

LIFESPAN 60-70 years

CONSERVATION STATUS

SOUTH AMERICA

Manatees are protected in many areas. All three species are endangered. One of the greatest threats they face is from the loss of their habitat to human development.

Because manatees have few predators, they are very relaxed and peaceful, despite their size.

Social life

Manatees are **solitary** animals who sometimes form small groups. Because they are so big they have few predators, other than man, and so have a very relaxed lifestyle and swim very slowly and gracefully. They are peaceful creatures and you are unlikely ever to see two manatees fighting.

After mating, males leave the females to give birth and rear the calf alone. Young manatee calves suckle from the mother until old enough to feed themselves.

Manatees are able to spend more than 24 minutes underwater at any one time.

FASCINATING FACTS

- A manatee can stay underwater for over 24 minutes. Watch the clock for 24 minutes and you'll realise how long that is!

- The name Trichechidae comes from the manatee's large hairy upper lip (The Greek word *trich* means 'hair').

- Because many of the water plants manatees eat are very tough, they have developed a very special way of replacing worn-down teeth. New teeth form at the back of the jaw and migrate forwards over time - as if they were on a very slow conveyor belt.

- Manatees have a very slow metabolism. This is useful if they ever get stranded in an area of shallow water (e.g. after a flood has receded) and have to go without food until they find their way back into the sea.

- Manatees are sometimes used as a natural form of weed control. They are placed in areas where weeds are a problem and happily munch their way through the plants until they have cleared them all.

Below: Manatees are so friendly that it is possible for humans to swim with them safely.

the lion: king of the beasts

CLASS	Mammalia
ORDER	Carnivora
FAMILY	Felidae
GENUS	*Panthera*
SPECIES	*leo*

In close up

I have worked with lions in the wild, in Africa, and watched them hunting on the **savannah** and sleeping in the shade of African trees (like the umbrella-shaped acacias). One of the **lionesses** didn't have a name, so she was named after me, because she was big and blonde.

The first things I think of when I picture a lion are the golden coat, the male's mane, enormous paws (much bigger than my hand) and muscular body. Lions purr like our cats do, but a lion's roar is far louder than a cat's meow! They have the same **scent glands** in their cheeks to mark territories with and both have excellent **nocturnal** vision. But, unlike many pets, lions have clean teeth. A natural diet of hide and bones obviously helps a lot if you don't brush your teeth every day (and lions don't). Lion teeth are also very sharp – all the better to kill their **prey** with. But the biggest difference has to be the size – I would be squashed flat if a lion tried to sit on my lap!

Lions are also found in India, where they are called Asiatic

Lions are very similar to domestic cats, but they have bigger teeth and a much louder ROAR!

lions. The main difference between the two is that Asiatic lions have a large shaggy mane on the belly and shoulders.

If you have a pet cat you will know it likes to scratch the furniture in your house. In the wild, lions also scratch their claws on soft wood. This keeps the claws sharp by removing dead nail from the tip (the cat equivalent of a manicure). It is important for cats to keep their claws in tip-top condition, so to stop your pet clawing all over the furniture see if you can find something that will make a good scratching post for it to use instead.

It isn't just the furniture cats scratch either! It can be

In Africa lionesses do most of the hunting, but after a major kill they may not hunt again for five or six days.

painful when my pet kitten jumps on my lap and starts 'paddling' (digging its claws in my legs). She does this because kittens 'paddle' on

their mother's tummy to get her to produce more milk. Domestic cats never totally grow up and kittens and adult cats alike affectionately claw at their owners before settling down to sleep. It is a habit they never grow out of.

Habitat

Lions are **terrestrial** and used to roam over all of Africa, but now they are confined to conservation areas in sub-Saharan Africa. The largest populations today can be found in East Africa (where Trude the **lioness** lives with her cubs) and the Kruger National Park in South Africa. There is also a small population of 200 Asiatic Lions in the Gir Forest Reserve in India.

Diet

Lions are **carnivores**. Few animals are too big for a

Life in a pride is very sociable.

WILD STATS

- **LENGTH** 170-190 cm (males) 140-175 cm (females)
- **HEIGHT** 80-110 cm
- **WEIGHT** 150-250 kg (males), 120-180 kg (females)
- **LIFESPAN** 12-15 years (up to 25 years in captivity)

CONSERVATION STATUS

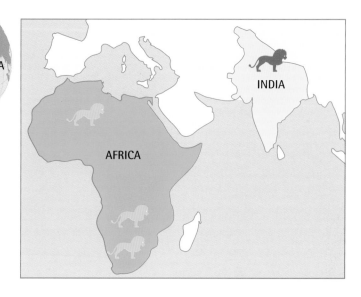

Lion populations in both Africa and Asia are in decline. The main threats to many lions are being killed by poachers and loss of habitat. The Asiatic lions of the Gir Forest Reserve and the African lions which live in National Parks are protected.

determined lion – even giraffes, young elephants, rhinoceroses and the odd hippopotamus may be on the menu! I once saw two lionesses hunting buffalo and another two kill a wart hog. Both times they killed their victim by biting the neck and strangling them. Despite their larger size, male lions carry out little of the hunting. The lionesses hunt in groups and this means they can catch larger animals. Personally, I would love a male who could catch his own food!

Lions tend to specialise in one type of **prey**, and, although it sounds horrible, I have seen a human finger and even a wallet found in the stomach of a man-eating lion.

After a large meal lions will not eat again for five or six days. Well would you, if you had just eaten so much?

Social life

Lions are the only **social** cats and they live in **prides**. Males are **territorial** and they are both **diurnal** and **nocturnal**. Asiatic lions tend to be more solitary, like domestic cats. They hunt alone and, luckily for the females, the males catch their own food.

Tired? Yes he may be, as lions sleep at least 20 hours a day!

By watching lions in the wild I have learnt a lot about how the cats I meet in the surgery behave. Lion **prides** consist of family members who hunt together to kill large animals. Watch your own cat hunting and stalking its **prey** and you will realise you are living with a lion. Although domestic cats are naturally **solitary**, when they are fed by their owner they no longer have to fight for food and so become **social**. The importance of family also explains why domestic cats will tolerate each other if they have been brought up together but will attack newcomers to their territory (your house and garden) once they are older.

Lions breed throughout the year. The females leave the pride to give birth, and produce 3 or 4 cubs per litter after a gestation period of between 110-116 days. Aren't they lovely?

5 — FASCINATING FACTS —

- The Lion is known as the King of the Beasts.

- Did you know the cub of a male tiger and female lion is known as a 'tigon', and if you swapped them around you would get a 'liger'!

- The lion is the second largest cat, after the tiger, and is the largest African carnivore.

- Lions doze for a staggering 20 hours a day!

- Two male lions, known as the Man-Eaters of Tsavo killed and ate over 40 railway workers in Kenya during the nineteenth century. Other man-eating lions killed and ate 84 people in Uganda in 1920, 22 people in East Africa in 1938 and 40 people in Zimbabwe in 1943. Man, however, is more often the predator than the **prey** since lions are naturally shy and are more likely to run away than attack you.

happy as a hyrax

CLASS	Mammalia
ORDER	Hyracoidea
FAMILY	Procaviidae

GENUS 3 genera: *Procavia* (rock hyrax) *Heterohyrax* (bush hyrax) *Dendrohyrax* (tree hyrax)

SPECIES 10 species

WILD STATS

PREDATORS	birds of **prey**
HEIGHT	15–25 cm
LENGTH	32–60 cm
WEIGHT	1.35–4 kg
LIFESPAN	9–14 years

In close up

They may look like rodents but these hairy creatures are most closely related to elephants. In the surgery I get to look at animals closely. If you look very closely at the pictures here you will see that the hyrax has small hooves. Because they climb trees and rocks a lot they also have elastic pads on the soles of their feet to help them grip better. Their thick grey-brown fur has longer black hairs. These are sensitive (like a cat's whiskers) and help hyraxes feel their way around in dark cracks between rocks.

As they are prone to parasites, hyraxes spend a lot of time grooming themselves using a special grooming claw on the back foot. This is the hyrax's equivalent of washing – and they never forget to wash behind their ears.

I met a wild hyrax when I was in Tsavo National Park in Africa. I felt a tugging at my trouser leg and when I looked down I saw a cheeky little hyrax peering back up at me. He reminded me of a large rat. But this particular hyrax was very bold and survived by begging off tourists. He was so cute it was hard to resist, and over the next few days I saw lots of people feeding him.

Rock hyraxes are the most common species, so named because they live in the mountains.

Habitat

Hyraxes are mainly found in sub-Saharan Africa. You can tell from the names which kind of terrain each type of hyrax likes to live in. Rock and bush hyraxes are **terrestrial** and tree hyraxes are **arboreal**.

Since hyraxes do a lot of climbing it's important that they can grip on tightly with the soles of their feet. They have an amazing way of clinging on – they can create a 'suction cup' with their feet. You can try this yourself: press the palms of your hands together tightly and then try and pull them apart – can you feel a force holding them together (and a rude noise)? This is exactly how hyraxes cling to rocks.

Diet

Hyraxes are **herbivores**. They eat leaves from bushes and other low-growing plants, as well as grass. Tree hyraxes get their leaves from taller bushes and trees.

Their ability to cling on to whatever they stand on makes hyraxes incredibly adaptable to their environment. This agile fellow is actually a bush hyrax.

- The name hyrax is, in fact, a mistake. Hyrax means 'shrew' as these animals were mistakenly identified as close relatives of the shrew.

- Hyraxes have been plagued by mistaken identity. Some 3,000 years ago an area of land containing hyrax-like rabbits was named Ishaphan – the 'land of the hyraxes'. The Romans later called it Hispania, and we know it today as Spain – and yet there are no hyraxes in Spain.

- Hyraxes are so tasty that one kind of eagle eats nothing but hyraxes.

- Hyraxes are the only mammals with hooves that are good climbers, and all thanks to suction.

- Like the rest of us, hyraxes love to play – especially in puddles. They slide sideways into the water, wallow about for a while, play with each other and then dry off with a spot of sunbathing. I think I would enjoy being a hyrax.

Hyraxes are home-loving creatures and rarely stray far from shelter.

Social life

Rock and bush hyraxes are **diurnal** while tree hyraxes are **nocturnal**. They live in family units made up of a **territorial** male with one or more females (sometimes as many as 17) and young. Female hyraxes give birth to just one young, although twins are sometimes born. Young males eventually leave the mother and move to a new **territory** while young females tend to stay close to the mother throughout their life. Hyraxes are **social** creatures and huddle together to keep warm. Like me, they like to lie in the sun to soak up some heat as well!

Hyraxes often bask in sunshine in the morning before going off to feed. During this time one animal will always keep watch.

CONSERVATION STATUS

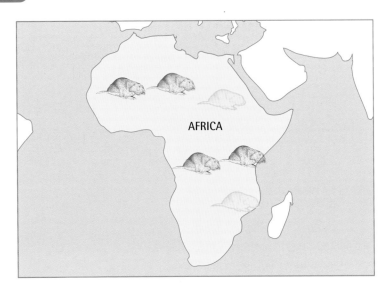

AFRICA

AFRICA

Some tree hyraxes are at risk due to hunting and loss of habitat, but rock and bush hyraxes are not at risk.

whale of a time

CLASS	Mammalia
ORDER	Cetacea
FAMILY	Balaenidae
GENUS	*Balaenoptera*
SPECIES	*musculus* (blue whale)

In close up

The blue whale is the largest mammal in the world. It moves like a living torpedo and because it spends its whole life underwater it is **aquatic**. A mammal the size of a blue whale could only live in the oceans where the water supports its enormous bulk.

Blue whales have gigantic mouths – you could easily jump around in one, and it would be safe, too, because they have no teeth. They are powerful swimmers and swim half-way around the globe between their birth grounds and feeding grounds.

Being so big you would think it was hard to miss seeing a blue whale. But looking for one is like looking for a needle in a haystack. One day I hope to go on a whale safari. It will be a very different experience to my African safari, but I am sure it will be just as exciting.

From the surface, one of the most dramatic views of a whale is when it dives in search of food.

A whale breathes through a blow hole in the top of its head.

Habitat

Blue whales swim between cold polar waters and warmer waters where their calves are born. Since the oceans cover two-thirds of the Earth's surface this is a very long distance indeed. Because whales cannot breathe underwater (like fish can) they have to come to the surface. Whales do not have nostrils like you or I; instead they have a blow hole in the top of their head.

Diet

Funnily enough, the largest mammals in the world feed on the tiniest plankton and shrimps. Whales swim with their mouths open, collecting organisms in the water. They then close their enormous mouths, expelling water through a fringe of **baleen plates** which form a filter. Because their food is so small whales are constantly swallowing and manage to eat four tons of plankton a day (that is more than any other mammal in the world).

Social life

Blue whales are **social** and spend most of their time in small **pods** of three to five animals, although they occasionally form larger groups. Whales give birth to one calf at a time. It probably won't surprise you that blue whale calves are the largest babies on Earth. But did you know they grow 1,000 times faster than a human baby in the womb, weigh two to three tons when born and drink 360 pints of milk a day? Like all mammals, whales suckle their young: the calf suckles as it swims alongside its mother.

Whales 'sing'. This is how they communicate with each other, but humans cannot hear them without special equipment. Whales can hear each other from a distance of over 800 kilometres!

- At one time blue whales were the most hunted because they contained the most blubber (used as fuel) and the longest whalebones (used to make corsets).

- Aristotle (350 BC) classed the whale as a fish due to its aquatic lifestyle. It was not until 1693 that the whale was recognised as a true mammal.

- The heart of a blue whale is as large as a small car! And the vessels leading to it are so big you could crawl through them.

What a mouthful! Air bubbles and water escape through the baleen plates of a blue whale's mouth.

- Whales are so good at swimming that even boat designers have studied their shape to make better ships.

- Whales don't blow water out of their blow hole: they blow air out. The air condenses and creates a spray – this is what you see. Whales can blow this spray up to a height of nine metres. Whale trackers and watchers use this spray for sighting **pods** in the distance.

WILD STATS

PREDATORS	humans and killer whales
LENGTH	25–35 metres (longest animal on Earth)
WEIGHT	80,000–135,000 kg (heaviest animal on Earth)
LIFESPAN	30–50 years

CONSERVATION STATUS

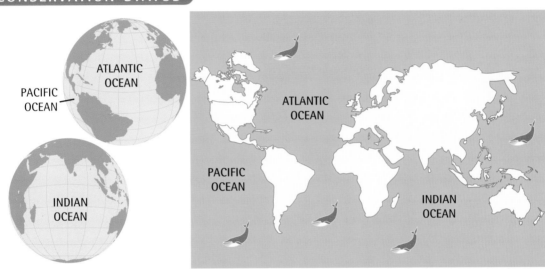

Blue whales are rare and were driven to the brink of extinction by whalers who hunted them for their blubber and bone. Conservation efforts have restored numbers to 10,000 animals.

At 25–35 metres the blue whale is the longest animal on Earth.

monkey mischief

CLASS	Mammalia		
ORDER	Primates		
FAMILY	Callitrichidae	Cercopithecidae	
GENUS	*Leontopithecus*	*Papio*	*Colobus*
SPECIES	*rosalia* lion tamarin	*hamadryas* (5 species) hamadryas baboon	*guereza* black & white colobus

Colobus monkeys are unique in that they have no thumbs.

In close up

In my travels I have met lots of different monkeys, each as fascinating and beautiful as the next. There are too many species to talk about here, but there are a few that stick out in my mind.

The first thing that struck me about the golden lion tamarin was its golden-yellow fur. These small monkeys really do live up to their name. And they even have a mane like a lion. They leap between trees in search of food, and once they spot a tasty morsel they move with such speed you can hardly keep track of them. Another meal they enjoy is tree sap, which they lick off the bark while clinging onto the trunk with their sharp claws.

Marmosets are very like tamarins. The pygmy marmoset is the smallest primate in the marmoset family and is as small as a mouse! Marmosets and tamarins come in all shapes and colours. Because they are so good at jumping about in the trees I think of them as the birds of the monkey world!

Tamarins have claws on their hands while other primates, like baboons and colobus monkeys, have fingernails like you and I. Baboons have huge sharp teeth which look very frightening and can give you a very nasty bite. I once had a tug-of-war with a baboon when I was in Kenya, Africa. I was sitting down drinking some coffee when a baboon jumped on the table and grabbed hold of the sugar bowl. I tried to grab it back and we ended up pulling it backwards and forwards between us. Then the baboon bared his teeth at me and I quickly gave in!

Another memorable monkey encounter was with the black and white colobus monkeys who also live in Kenya. A new road had been built through the monkeys' home range. Because colobus monkeys are leaf-eaters they spend most of their time in trees and are slow and cumbersome on the ground. They were so slow that cars were running them over whenever they tried to cross the road. So we placed ladders across the road, high up in the trees on either side of it. Once the colobus monkeys got used to the new ladders they would happily play about on them for hours and could once again move safely through their territory.

Habitat

Tamarins and marmosets live in the forests of South America. Like most monkeys, they are **arboreal**. Colobus monkeys and baboons live in Africa. Like the tamarins and marmosets, colobus monkeys are also **arboreal**, while baboons spend most of their time on ground and are **terrestrial**.

Diet

Tamarins and marmosets are **omnivores**. They eat insects, spiders, fruits, tree sap, flowers, leaves, nectar, lizards, birds' eggs and tree frogs. Colobus monkeys are **herbivores** and feed only on leaves. Baboons, as I found out, will eat just about any-thing and will quite happily eat tourists' picnic food as well as their natural **herbivorous** diet of fruit and leaves.

Social life

Tamarins and marmosets are **social** and **diurnal** and live in family groups of two to twenty individuals. Male tamarins make very good fathers and help carry the young whenever they can. This is a good job because otherwise the female would really have her hands full.

Male tamarins and marmosets tend not to fight. Instead, they stare each other out, until one gives in.

A pygmy marmoset – the smallest in the primate family.

Overall, they are peace-loving animals and youngsters are always eager to help look after their baby brothers and sisters. Lion tamarins, the largest tamarins, usually give birth to one or two young, and occasionally three.

WILD STATS

PREDATORS cats, birds of **prey** and snakes (tamarins and marmosets), leopards, lions hyenas, pythons and eagles (hamadryas baboons)

LENGTH 20–33.5 cm (tamarins and marmosets), 45–70 cm (black and white colobus monkeys), 50–94 cm (hamadryas baboons)

WEIGHT 380–700 g (tamarins and marmosets), 6.5–14.5 kg (black and white colobus monkeys), 10–18k g (hamadryas baboons)

LIFESPAN over 10 years (tamarins and marmosets), 25 years (black and white colobus monkeys), 40 years (hamadryas baboons)

FASCINATING FACTS

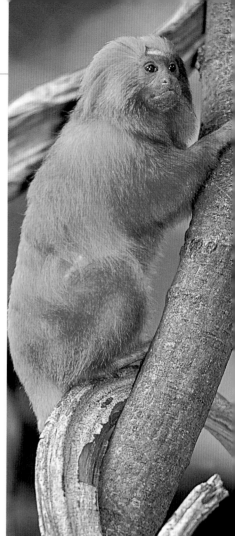

- Tamarins are also known as 'squirrel monkeys' because they move like squirrels through the trees.

- Did you know that some monkeys even live in the snow. Japanese macaques or 'snow monkeys' live in the mountains of Japan. In the winter, when it is *really* cold, the macaques take warm baths in hot springs to heat themselves up.

- There are hundreds of different kinds of monkeys. The noisiest is the howler monkey which lives in Central and South America. Their 'howls' can be heard over five kilometres away!

- While lion tamarins are on the brink of extinction there is still some hope for the future. Projects in Brazil have been breeding golden lion tamarins (like the one pictured on the right) in captivity and releasing them back into the wild successfully. Before release the monkeys have to be trained in how to live naturally, even down to such small details as how to gather food.

- If you want to see lots of monkeys in one place then South America is the place to go. More monkeys live there than anywhere else in the world.

CONSERVATION STATUS

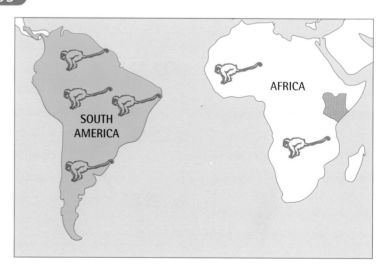

Most tamarin species, including the golden lion tamarin, are threatened with extinction by destruction of their habitat.

apeing the apes

CLASS	Mammalia
ORDER	Primates
FAMILY	Pongidae
GENUS	*Pan* *Gorilla*
SPECIES	*troglodytes* *gorilla*

Of all the apes, chimpanzees possess the most human-like qualities.

In close up

Of all the mammals, the apes are the most closely related to us. And of all the apes it is the chimpanzee that reminds me the most of humans. You only have to look at a chimpanzee and you will notice how human-like its features are. Like us they are **terrestrial**, but spend a lot of time in trees since this is where much of their food can be found. Gorillas are also **terrestrial** and spend even more of their time on the ground.

I once had a close encounter with the mountain gorillas in Bwindi, Africa. Two silverbacks – large males – had been fighting and one had cuts all down his back. There was nothing a vet like myself could do for him because treating large wild animals can be very dangerous and so we left the wounds to heal by themselves. It never ceases to surprise me how robust wild animals are and how quickly their wounds can heal.

For me, seeing the mountain gorillas was a life-long dream come true. It was amazing to come so close to them and they spent as much time watching us as we did them. What I didn't realise was that gorillas break wind all the time! This is because of all the leaves they eat. The adults were very relaxed with us and the infants and teenagers were really cheeky – just like human children. One sneaked up behind us and jumped out at the last minute. I couldn't believe how human-like they were. It makes me very sad to think these incredible animals are being killed off by poachers. They are also suffering because of the war in Central Africa. Their habitat is shrinking at an alarming rate and their future looks bleak.

Chimpanzees are smaller than gorillas, but still bigger than I first imagined. They have sparse black hair over most of the body and females develop large pink swellings to signal to the males when they are ready to mate. Like humans, female chimpanzees generally give birth to just one baby.

Chimpanzees walk on all fours, but can also walk like humans do – on two legs. If you look closely at a chimpanzee in the zoo you will see it pulls faces, much like a human does and this is one way in which they communicate. For humans, it is often easier to tell that a friend is unhappy by looking at their face than by talking to them. Chimpanzees can do this, too. They can show 'human' emotions like joy, grief or anger. But, despite research into the possibility, chimpanzees have not been taught to talk!

Habitat

Chimpanzees are found in sub-Saharan Africa. They live in rainforests and on **savannahs** which have sufficient tree cover. Because the ground is a dangerous place to be (with leopards prowling around) chimpanzees sleep in trees. Having nails, like humans do, they cannot cling onto branches while they are asleep like tree sloths can and so they build nests. These nests are a bit like temporary tree houses and look very comfortable.

Gorillas live in Central Africa, in the mountains and lowland swamps. Because they are the largest mammals in that part of the world they can quite happily sleep on the ground as they have no predators to avoid.

Diet

Chimpanzees are **omnivores**. They eat fruits, leaves, nuts, bark, seeds, **termites**, ants and small mammals. Sometimes they even eat other monkeys! Chimpanzees are clever animals when it comes to solving problems – especially when food is involved. Can you imagine eating without a knife and fork? Obviously, chimps do not have knives and forks. Instead, they use sticks to fish for termites and leaves to soak up water, like a sponge, which they then drip into their mouths. Some chimpanzees have even learnt to crush the hard shells of nuts with large stones!

Gorillas are **herbivores**. They eat shoots and leaves by the bucketload! In fact, they spend most of their time eating.

Social life

Chimpanzees are incredibly **social** animals. They live in large groups (with anything from 30 to 100 animals) which split up into smaller groups during the day to forage for food – so we call them **diurnal**. They spend a lot of time grooming one another and this helps build friendships. Like you, chimpanzees love playing with each other and this

---

WILD STATS

PREDATORS	leopards hunt chimpanzees and humans poach apes for their meat
HEIGHT	70–170 cm chimpanzees, 140–185 cm gorillas
WEIGHT	45 kg (males), 33 kg (females) chimpanzees
	33–47 kg (males), 43–60 kg (females) gorillas
LIFESPAN	40–50 years chimpanzees
	40–50 years gorillas

A chimpanzee's face is as expressive as a human's. How do you think this one's feeling?

Gorillas are the largest of the primates, but they exist on a diet of shoots, leaves and fruits.

5 FASCINATING FACTS

- Chimpanzees have been taught to communicate with humans using sign language.

Handprint

Footprint

- Chimpanzee hands look very much like yours and mine. Place your hand next to the handprint opposite and you will see how similar they are. How does your hand differ in shape? If you spent all day in trees do you think it would help to have longer fingers, like a chimpanzee?

- Now look at the footprint – does it look more like your foot or your hand? Having a big toe that acts like a thumb means chimpanzees have an extra pair of hands when climbing around in trees.

- The gorilla is the largest ape of all – a staggering 1.8 metres tall and weighing up to 175 kg!

- The largest ape ever was called *Gigantopithecus* and was much bigger than the gorilla at 2.75 metres tall and weighing an amazing 272 kg!

CONSERVATION STATUS

AFRICA

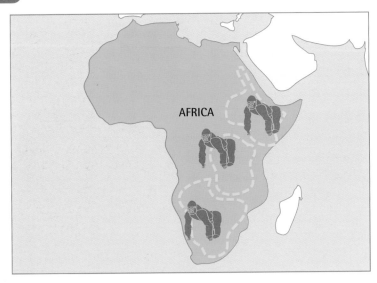

AFRICA

- - - - - Mountain regions

Endangered by destruction of habitat and by hunting.

teaches them skills they will need when they are adults.

The group is led by an **alpha male**. He is the 'King' of the group, but has to keep his position by scaring off other males. The **alpha male** mates with most of the females, although young males will often go to ingenious lengths to mate with females behind the **alpha male's** back.

When chimpanzees fight their hair stands up on end. It makes them look bigger than they are and is meant to scare off their rival. I see this a lot in the cats that come into the surgery when they are frightened. Look at your cat next time it has been in a fight or had a scare and you will see what I mean.

Gorillas are also **social** mammals. They live in smaller groups than chimpanzees and are also **diurnal**. The dominant male in a gorilla group is called the silverback, because he has a silver back, and is usually absolutely enormous! He lives with several females and young and will protect them from any danger, which is normally in the form of poachers.

A gorilla group is dominated by the silverback – usually the biggest male in the group.

the perfect pangolin

CLASS Mammalia
ORDER Pholidota
FAMILY Manidae
GENUS *Manis*
SPECIES Seven species

In close up

The pangolin is special because it is the only mammal to have scales. Like a medieval knight in his suit of armour, these scales offer plenty of protection. When threatened by a **predator** pangolins roll up into a ball and stay in this shape by locking their scales onto one another – I tried to prise one open once and couldn't manage it. I like to

When threatened, a pangolin will curl up into a tight ball to protect itself from harm.

think of them as the armoured tanks of the animal kingdom.

All pangolins are good climbers, and some are even champion swimmers. Because pangolins are **nocturnal**, they have poor eyesight. Instead, they rely on a terrific sense of smell – and they are particularly good at picking up the smell of the **termites** and ants they feed on.

Habitat

Pangolins live in the **savannahs** and forests of Asia and Africa. They are **territorial** and mark their **territory** with **scent** sprayed from special **glands**. Both **arboreal** and **terrestrial**, they can move just as easily on the ground as up in the trees.

Diet

Pangolins feed on **termites** and ants. The larger species may also eat other insects. Pangolins have no teeth. Instead, they suck up termites and ants using their tongue and long snout. Some ants and **termites** bite when angry and the pangolin's armour is designed to prevent this. But sometimes ants crawl under the scales to the soft skin. If this happens pangolins have another means of defence 'up their scales'. They can grind their scales together, crushing the ants underneath to death. Young pangolins first learn to eat by picking out insects from between the mother's scales.

Look at the pictures of aardvarks on page 18-21. Can you see the similarities? Notice that aardvarks also have a long snout, long head and strong front digging legs. All these features are essential to finding and feeding on ants and termites.

Social life

Pangolins are **solitary**. Most pangolins are **nocturnal** (although the long-tailed pangolin is **diurnal**). Females give birth to one young at a time and they travel around on the mother's back by clinging onto the scales.

CONSERVATION STATUS

Pangolins are under threat in both African and Asia. Their main problem is loss of habitat and because they are the victims of poachers.

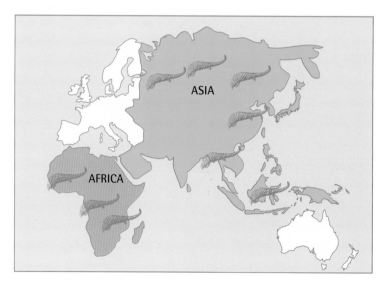

PREDATORS	few predators can crush the hard scaley covering. Leopards and pythons pose the biggest threat
LENGTH	35 cm (long-tailed pangolin), 90 cm (giant pangolin)
WEIGHT	1.2 kg (long-tailed pangolin), 30 kg (giant pangolin)
LIFESPAN	unknown in the wild, 4.5 years in captivity

(Left) The end of a pangolin's quest – a huge termite mound full of food.

5 FASCINATING FACTS

- Pangolins are sometimes called 'living pine cones' or 'pineapples'. The name Pangolin is French and means 'roller' because they roll up into a ball.

- The scales of pangolins are made of hairs that have been cemented together.

- The pangolin tongue is extraordinarily long, measuring up to 18 cm.

- As they have no teeth, pangolins crush their **prey** using their stomachs – so their stomachs do all the chewing.

- The long-tailed pangolin has more bones in its tail than any other mammal.

Pangolins eat termites and ants – and a tongue like this (which reminds me of a stick of rhubarb) helps suck them up from their hiding places. A pangolin tongue can be up to 18 cm long.

rhinoceroses: tons of fun

CLASS	Mammalia
ORDER	Perissodactyla
FAMILY	Rhinocerotidae

GENUS	*Ceratotherium*	*Diceros*	*Rhinoceros*	*Dicerorhinus*
SPECIES	*simum*	*bicornis*	*unicornis sondaicus*	*sumatrensis*
	(white rhino)	(black rhino)	(Indian & Javan)	(Sumatran)

These female white rhinos from Longleat have formed a small temporary group, despite normally being solitary animals.

In close up

The first time I saw a wild rhino was in Zimbabwe, in Africa. I met five black rhino calves, and I couldn't believe how big they were. They were so heavy and solid they looked and felt like large blocks of concrete. It was only the little eyes peeping out that made them look alive. Like all children, they were cheeky and liked to play games. Their favourite game was to push me over. After a while I learnt to be firm with them (I had to herd them like sheep, using a stick), but I still ended up with bruises all over me.

The cheekiest rhino actually saved my life. One day I took the calves for a walk down to a lake for a drink. Suddenly I heard someone shout 'buffalo' and turned around to see some buffaloes charging towards us. There were crocodiles in the lake and nowhere for us to run. Then one of the rhino calves charged out of the bushes, squealing like a puppy, and chased the buffaloes away. She obviously felt very protective towards us because she guarded us for the rest of the day. We were much better friends after that, but I found it very funny that such a large animal could make such a high-pitched squeaky noise.

Some rhinoceroses have one horn (Indian and Javan) and others two horns (black, white and Sumatran) on their nose. These horns are used as head weapons when rhinos fight with each other or defend themselves against attackers. If you get as close to a rhino as I did you will see how huge and solid they are. They have very little hair but they do have hairy tufts at the ends of their ears. The odd one out is the Sumatran rhinoceros. With its red-brown fur it looks a bit like a woolly mammoth.

Because male rhinoceroses fight using their horns they have very thick skin to protect themselves from each other. By looking at a rhinoceros it is hard to guess which other mammals they are most closely related to. Would you be surprised if I told you it is the horse? And would you believe the very first rhinoceroses looked like dog-sized horses.

Habitat

Rhinos need a lot of space to roam, especially the black and white rhinos that live on the open plains of Africa. The Indian rhinoceros lives on the open plains of India, and the Javan and Sumatran rhinoceros live in the forests of Asia.

Diet

Winston, a male white rhino, just loves bread, bagels and croissants.

Although they look like big and ferocious killers rhinos are **herbivores**. Plain-dwelling rhinos eat grass, while those who live in forests eat twigs and bushes. All the rhinos have a flexible upper lip which helps them pick the most nutritious parts of the plants. During the dry season

WILD STATS

PREDATORS humans. Black and white rhino young may be preyed upon by lions and hyenas. Indian, Javan and Sumatran rhino young may be preyed upon by tigers and hyenas

HEIGHT 1.35–1.85 metres

LENGTH 2.6–3.8 metres

WEIGHT 0.8–2.3 tons

LIFESPAN 35–45 years

African rhinos travel long distances in search of water.

The white rhinos at Longleat have a sweet tooth. It is funny to watch cream buns and doughnuts disappearing into their wide mouths. We have to feed them these to get them to stand still so I can take blood samples: after all, it isn't easy to get an animal as large as a rhinoceros to stand still without some kind of reward.

Social life

Rhinos like to spend a lot of time alone and so are classed as **solitary**. However, sometimes they form small, temporary groups, like the ones at Longleat.

Female rhinos give birth to one young at a time and mother and calf are very close for several years until the young rhino is able to look after itself. Rhinos find an area with lots of food and then protect it from other animals and so are **territorial**.

To communicate with each other rhinos use sound and smell. Rhinos have very poor eyesight and cannot see long distances, so they rely on **scent-marking** to let each other know where their **territories** are. The black rhinoceros does this by trampling fresh dung with its hind feet. This leaves a scent trail which other rhinos can follow. The Javan and Indian rhinoceros mark their paths with **scented** liquid produced by a **scent-gland** on the back of the foot.

This is the lovely rhino that saved my life in Zimbabwe by chasing off a buffalo.

CONSERVATION STATUS

All five rhino species are threatened with extinction due to loss of their habitat and poaching for their horns.

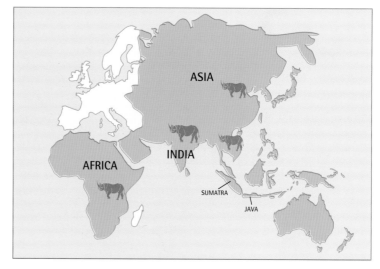

- Powdered rhinoceros horn is sold as a medicine in the Far East. Scientists have tested it and found it has no effect, yet this superstition has led to the near extinction of these amazing animals.

- A group of rhinoceroses is called a 'crash'.

- As a result of hunting by humans rhinos have recently developed two new alarm calls to warn each other of danger. This is just one way in which humans have changed the behaviour of wild animals.

- There are so few Javan rhinos left in the wild it is the rarest species of large mammal in the world.

- The black and white rhinoceroses are neither black nor white! In fact the names arose from a misunderstanding: both are named after the shapes of their lips, and this is the easiest way to tell them apart. 'White' comes from the **Boer** word 'wijde' or 'wide' to describe the white rhino's wide lips. The black rhino is not black at all but grey and has a 'hook lip'. It is also known as the 'hook-lipped' rhinoceros.

White rhinos' heads are so heavy that they are usually carried only a few centimetres from the ground.

camels: one hump or two?

CLASS	Mammalia
ORDER	Artiodactyla
FAMILY	Camelidae
GENUS	*Camelus*
SPECIES	*dromedarius* (one-humped or dromedary camel)
	ferus (two-humped or Bactrian camel)

In close up

If you or I were to spend more than a few hours in the desert we would **dehydrate**. That is why, when I am out in such arid environments, I have to take lots of water with me.

But camels have a much smarter way of dealing with this problem: they store water and energy (in the form of fat) in their humps. Camels are **terrestrial**, and have long legs to carry them across the vast expanse of the deserts in which they live. They have a thick woolly coat (pelage) and a long neck (though not as long as the giraffe).

The first time I came across wild camels was in Africa. I had to **castrate** some males, but in order to get near them I first had to make friends with them. Camels recognise each other by bleating like sheep and the males make a whistling sound by grinding their teeth together. To introduce myself I let them sniff and nuzzle my face gently – that is how you say 'hello' to a camel. But I had to be very careful because camels can bite and after greeting the last one he ate my hat.

To get a camel to stand still you have to tie its legs together, and this is when

Camels are quite friendly, but it is important to introduce yourself properly to gain their trust.

Camels are known as 'ships of the desert' because of their durability in hostile weather.

things started to get hairy. Suddenly, my peaceful new friend turned into a spitting monster with a green tongue and yellow teeth. He was making some very frightening noises and I was glad when the whole ordeal was over.

Habitat

Camels can be found in the desert and **steppe** regions of Arabia and North Africa. Have you noticed that sand is difficult to walk through? Camels have large padded feet that make walking easier

and they also have a special way of walking – watch a dog or cat walking and you will notice that they move the front and back leg from opposite sides of the body at the same time. Camels move the front and back legs on the same side at the same time – this is what makes

them sway from side to side. They will quite happily pull a cart, much like a horse would in this country, for kilometres at a time and they don't even mind when the weather is bad: in a sand storm they can close their nostrils, while their long, double eyelashes keep sand out of their eyes.

WILD STATS

PREDATORS	none
HEIGHT	180–230 cm
WEIGHT	600–1,000 kg
LIFESPAN	40 years

My camel friends at Longleat, like all other camels, are not fussy about what they eat.

Diet

Camels are **herbivores**. They cannot afford to be fussy because there is very little choice of food in the desert, so they will eat any plants they can find – even thorny shrubs – ouch! They have four-chambered stomachs (like cows) and can eat otherwise inedible foods. They can go for days, and even weeks, without drinking, relying instead on liquid from the fat in their humps and in their food. You would be amazed to see how much water a camel can drink in one go. If any other mammal tried to drink as much water as a thirsty camel its blood cells would burst. But camels have a trick up their sleeve to deal with this: they have double the number of blood cells of any other mammal, so they can carry twice as much water in the blood.

Social life

Camels are highly **social** and live in family groups in the wild. During times of drought they may even form herds of several hundred individuals to undertake long migrations to far-off watering holes. Like giraffes and other migratory animals, they are not **territorial**.

- Camels were first domesticated between 4000 and 2000 BC. Man domesticated the camel because it makes the perfect desert pet. Not only are they useful for carrying heavy loads and producing energy rich milk (they can be milked like cows) but they can also be used for racing! Nothing is wasted: even camels' dung is so dry it can be used for fuel by the nomads who herd them!

- A camel's body temperature varies greatly – from 28° to 41°C, depending on the weather. This prevents it from losing valuable water as sweat. Try measuring your body temperature – you will find it stays the same almost all the time.

- The one-humped camel can produce 20 litres of milk from the fat stored in its hump and the water stored in its body tissues. That's a lot of liquid.

- Camels can lose almost 50 per cent of their body weight in water without harm. Just a 14 per cent loss in humans is fatal.

- The earliest fossil remains of camels were found in North America and showed the animals to be the size of rabbits!

Two-humped camels can produce 50 litres of milk from the fat and water stored in their body tissue.

CONSERVATION STATUS

Only Bactrian camels remain as wild animals, and even then there are only a few hundred individuals left, in the south of the Gobi desert, in Mongolia and China.

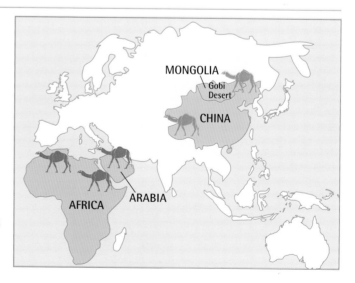

batty about bats

CLASS) Mammalia

ORDER) Chiroptera

FAMILY) 18 including Craseony-
cteridae and Pteropodidae

GENUS) 187 genera including
Craseonycteris

SPECIES) 950 including: 174 species
flying foxes, and *thonglongya*
(hog-nosed bat)

In close up

Bats are remarkable creatures, and are the only mammals to have conquered the skies. Able to fly long distances they have travelled over seas and oceans to reach faraway lands. When I was a child I thought they were birds, because they could fly, but now I know they are mammals.

There are a huge number of species of bats (950 in all). The order even includes the smallest known mammal – the hog-nosed bat – which is so small you can hold it in the palm of your hand with plenty of space to spare.

The largest bats are pretty big, and they are known as flying foxes because of their size. But they are not foxes at all. If you look at a flying fox closely you will see it is 100 per cent bat. You are probably familiar with the image of bats associated with Dracula: black, **nocturnal**, blood-sucking creatures. But most bats eat insects, and are known as **insectivores**, while others eat fruit and are called **frugivores**. Many bats are brownish in colour, but some of the flying foxes have striking coloured markings and I think they are rather beautiful.

How do bats fly? They have wings, but they are not like birds' wings with feathers. The arms and legs of bats have been modified: imagine a sheet of skin attached between your waist, wrist and ankles – now, if you flap your arms together, you can pretend you are a bat! Bats sleep hanging upside down. They grip onto a surface using their claws and do not relax this grip, even when fast asleep. Most bats are born with a full covering of hair. It's so cold in the caves they live in that they would freeze to death without it.

Habitat

The hog-nosed bat lives in caves alongside the River Kwai

A flying fox hanging around in a city park in India.

(in south-west Thailand). This is the only place it is found. Flying foxes live in the trees and caves of tropical forests in Africa, Asia and Australia, and can often be found hanging around in city parks!

You may even have bats living near you – keep an eye out at night and see if you can spot any. But you'll have to watch closely, because they fly very fast.

Diet

The hog-nosed bat is an **insectivore**, but because it is so small it can only eat very small insects. Flying foxes are **omnivores** and eat fruits, flowers, leaves, nectar, pollen and insects. Most bats hunt their **prey** at night, but because they have such poor eyesight they have to find their food another way: by **echo-location**. Bats send out special signals through their nose and mouth and this probably explains why they have such funny-looking faces. These signals echo off any obstacles, telling the bat where its **prey** is. This is similar to the sonar navigation system used by submarines. You can try this **echo-location** yourself, somewhere where you can make echoes (perhaps in a tunnel under a railway line, or in a cave or by a gorge). Shut your eyes and shout and see if you can work out where the echoes bounce back from first. You will probably find this very hard because you are not a bat.

WILD STATS

PREDATORS	humans and **nocturnal** birds of **prey**
LENGTH	3 cm (hog-nosed bats), up to 40 cm (flying foxes)
WEIGHT	1.5-3 g (hog-nosed bats), up to 1500 g (flying foxes)
WINGSPAN	13-17 cm (hog-nosed bats), almost 2 metres (flying foxes)
LIFESPAN	unknown (hog-nosed bats), up to 30 years (flying foxes)

A bat in flight is a wonderful sight. Note the long wings and brightly-coloured fur.

CONSERVATION STATUS

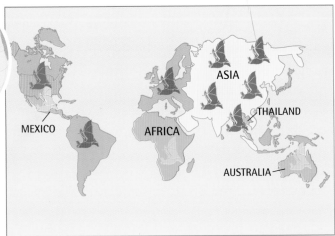

The hog-nosed bat is extremely rare, with a total population of only 200 left in the wild. Most bat populations are declining due to the destruction of their habitats by humans.

Social life

Bats are generally **social** animals, roosting as **colonies** in caves, although some species roost in curled-up leaves, under branches, in tree hollows and just about anywhere dark and sheltered. Bats hunt alone, returning to roost in the safety of numbers.

A bat's echo-location system is located in its nose and mouth – maybe that's why they look so funny.

5 FASCINATING FACTS

• Did you know that some bats go fishing? This is not for fun but to catch food – or fish, to be precise. So impressive is this method of hunting, the bats that do it have been named 'fisherman bats'. They use echo-location to 'see' fish and then swoop down and pluck their unfortunate **prey** from the water.

• Bats have the funniest looking faces in the whole mammal world – just look at the picture on the left.

• Vampire bats really do exist and they suck the blood of mammals, including humans. They can move on all-fours on the ground as they smell out their victim. To suck the blood the bat first bites its victim and then laps up the blood as it trickles out.

• One colony of Mexican free-tailed bats was so large that at one time it contained 100 million bats. I wonder who counted them all!

• The hog-nosed bat is so small no one noticed it until 30 years ago.

porky polar bears

CLASS	Mammalia
ORDER	Carnivora
FAMILY	Ursidae
GENUS	*Ursus*
SPECIES	*martimus*

In close up

I have to watch what I eat (I love ice-cream) or I put on weight. But polar bears have a different problem. It is vital for their survival that they're as fat as possible to keep warm. In the Arctic there is snow everywhere you look, it is bitterly cold and there are very few visible sources of food. Polar bears have their work cut out for them, hunting in that kind of terrain.

My sister lives in the Arctic, where some people choose to carry guns to go shopping – just in case they meet an aggressive polar bear. As cuddly as they look, these mammals can be deadly. Fortunately, polar bears do not travel as far south as Norway, where the rest of my family live, so I don't need to worry when I visit them.

Cuddly as they look, polar bears can be deadly for human beings.

On one visit to the enormous wasteland of the Arctic, we had to put radio collars on some polar bears to follow their movements. When I got near a **sedated** polar bear I was amazed at the enormous size of their broad feet, which act like snow-shoes on the ice and paddles for swimming in the water. Just as well, when you have to walk as far as a polar bear does every year to feed and mate. I also noticed webbing between their toes which helps them swim faster.

Habitat

Polar bears live in the Arctic (the North Pole). Because there is little shelter they have incredibly thick coats to keep them warm, and shiny yellowish-white fur to keep them camouflaged.

Diet

Polar bears are **carnivores** – the largest in the world – and they have to eat meat to survive in a land where very few plants can grow. They particularly like the thick blubber of seals. Because there may be long gaps between meals polar bears have to store the fat in their bodies, and the best place is on the **rump**.

Polar bears hunt seals by smelling them out as they rest in dens, and then jump on the ice above where the seal is hidden. They also wait by a breathing hole and drag the seal out by its nose when it comes up for air – ouch!

A hungry polar bear lies in wait by a seal's breathing hole.

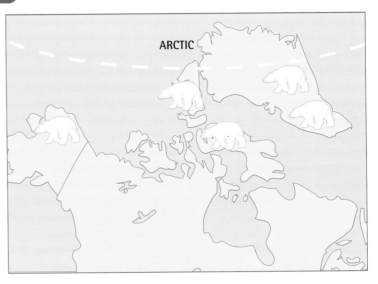

CONSERVATION STATUS

ARCTIC

ARCTIC

World population is estimated between 7,000 and 20,000.
Polar bears are protected in the Russian Arctic. North America and Scandinavia control hunting levels.

PREDATORS	who would dare pick a fight with the largest carnivore in the world? Only humans hunt polar bears
LENGTH	241-25 cm (males), 180-210 cm (females)
HEIGHT	up to 160 cm
WEIGHT	320-1000 kg
LIFESPAN	20-30 years in the wild, 40 years in captivity

Not only are polar bears enormous, but some of the animals they hunt are, too. Polar bears have killed and eaten walruses and even beluga whales.

Sometimes I wish I was a polar bear so I could spend all my days eating ice-cream.

Social life

Polar bears are **solitary** mammals. Males and females

A polar bear tucking into a big meaty meal – essential in the hostile environment in which they live.

Polar bear cubs stay with their mum for several years before leaving to forage for themselves.

do not stay together after mating and the female raises her two cubs alone. A male will sometimes kill the pups of a female he has never met before so he can mate with her.

Polar bears give birth in self-dug snow caves where they suckle the young during **hibernation**. The mother's body keeps the youngsters warm. When the cubs are big enough she must lead them out of the cave to the sea. For a year or two she trains them to hunt, and they learn to fight by playing with each other, before setting out in search of food or a mate.

• Before making the long trek to the mating ground the female polar bear fattens herself up to twice her normal body size.

• After giving birth (often to twins) the female polar bear suckles her cubs, going without food the whole time! Female polar bears often go without food for eight months of the year. It makes me hungry just thinking about it.

• Polar bear cubs must grow to ten times their birth weight before they can leave the den and venture out into the wild Arctic wasteland. But this isn't so difficult when your mother produces milk that is as fat-rich as cream (a staggering 50 per cent fat)

• Some polar bears cover their noses with snow when stalking seals on the open ice. You could say they were masters of disguise.

Above: A bear shields its face from an Arctic storm.
Right: Polar bears are the only bears to actively prey on humans. Scary huh?

• Polar bears are the only bears to actively prey on humans. The last recorded polar bear attack on a human occurred in 1995, when a tourist was killed by a sub-adult male. However, so many people carry firearms in the Arctic that polar bears usually come off worst in such confrontations.

a flight with flying lemurs

CLASS	Mammalia
ORDER	Dermoptera
FAMILY	Cynocephalidae
GENUS	*Cynocephalus*

In close up

Flying lemurs are creatures of habit. Each night they forage along the same routes through the trees and even have their own flightpaths which they guard against other flying lemurs. Because they live in trees they are **arboreal**. A sheet of skin stretches between the neck, fingertips, toes and tail, forming two 'wings'. These cat-sized animals use their 'wings' to glide between branches. They have white spots on a pale brown and reddish back, large eyes, a pointed snout, sharp, curved claws and small ears.

Habitat

Flying lemurs live in the rainforests of Indonesia and

When on the ground, these strange creatures resemble other small mammals you might find in the rainforest...

the Philippines. During the day they sleep in tree hollows, hanging upside down and clinging on with all four limbs. Like many **arboreal** mammals, they must cling tightly to branches while asleep so they don't fall off.

Diet

Flying lemurs are **herbivores**. They feed on leaves, buds, flowers and fruits which grow on the trees they live in.

Social life

Flying lemurs tend to be **solitary** creatures. They are **territorial** over sleeping places and landing platforms on trees. They are active at night and so are **nocturnal**.

... but in flight they are extraordinary, gliding between the trees with grace and accuracy, alighting where they want in seach of leaves, buds, flowers and fruit.

CONSERVATION STATUS

Flying lemurs are threatened due to the loss of their habitat to human developments.

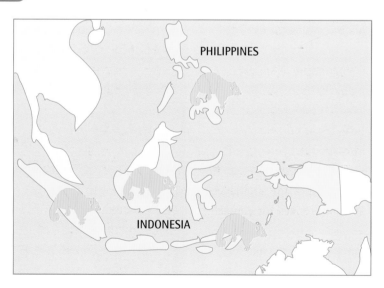

WILD STATS

PREDATORS	humans
HEIGHT	33–42 cm
WEIGHT	1–1.8 kg
LIFESPAN	17.5 years has been recorded in captivity before the flying lemur in question escaped!

The young hang on tight to mum's fur – it's a long way to fall from the canopy of the rainforest.

5 FASCINATING FACTS

- Flying lemurs are the largest gliding mammals on Earth.

- Flying lemurs have been a puzzle to scientists for years. They are similar to both bats and primates in may ways, and yet are different in others – see if you can spot the similarities and differences for yourself.

- The two sheets of skin between their arms and legs are used to glide between trees. The maximum distance recorded for a leap is 136 metres – that is longer than a football pitch!

- Watching a flying lemur going to the toilet is a comical sight. The creature hangs on to the side of a tree with its front legs, letting the back legs hang freely. It then arches its tail backwards and deposits its droppings. It is funny, but not if you're standing underneath!

- Because flying lemurs spend a lot of time hanging upside down under branches the young have an interesting sleeping place. They sit on their mother's tummy which forms a kind of furry hammock. Comfortable, and with a great view!

an elephant never forgets

CLASS Mammalia

ORDER Proboscideans

FAMILY Elephantidae

GENUS 2 genera: *Elephas*   *Loxidonta*

SPECIES 2 species: *maximus* (Asian)

africana (African)

In close up

The African elephant is the largest land mammal on earth. But how do you tell an African elephant from an Asian elephant? Well, it's easy. African elephants are larger than Asian elephants and have larger ears than their Asian cousins. The African elephant also has two 'grasping fingers' at the end of its trunk while the Asian elephant has just one. Female Asian elephants are the only elephants that do not have tusks. These tusks (which never stop growing) are actually massive incisors. Imagine if your front teeth were as big as an elephant's.

And talking of big, elephant feet are enormous: the footprints of an elephant cover a staggering one square metre. Get someone to show you how big this is and you will be amazed. Having such big feet spreads the elephant's weight out more evenly – but you still wouldn't want one to step on your toes!

I once got the chance to operate on an elephant in the wild. He was a massive bull elephant who was suffering from 'floppy trunk syndrome'. After **sedating** him I had to take a sample of muscle from his trunk. As I sat next to his mouth he almost blew me away with each breath. He

Right: An Asian elephant has smaller ears than its African cousin.
Below: The African elephant is the largest species of elephant and the largest living land animal.

was snoring so loudly, I didn't even hear another elephant when he crept up behind me to watch! Bull elephants are **solitary** and not protective of each other. However, had they been two females (cows) it would have been another story.

Just like me, elephants take care of their skin, only they do this by bathing and wallowing in mud, sand and dust. One time I had to treat an elephant at Longleat by spreading yoghurt over his skin. Look at this measure: an elephant's skin is 2 cm thick! Imagine wearing a skin that thick. How would you go about dislodging parasites and keeping clean and cool? You, too, would have to wallow in mud and water to clean yourself, and grow large flappable ears to cool yourself down with.

Because of their diet and their size, there are no predators for adult elephants, so they do not need to move quickly. In fact, there is nothing quite as majestic as a herd of elephants striding in slow motion across the African savannah, their trunks and tails (with hairs as thick as spaghetti) swaying from side to side.

2 cm

My friend Limbo, an eight-year-old African bull from Longleat.

Habitat

As the names suggest, Asian elephants live in Asia, while African elephants live in Africa. Both species are **terrestrial** but the African elephant prefers **savannahs**, plains and mountains while the Asian elephant prefers savannahs and forests.

Diet

Elephants are **herbivores**. They eat grasses, branches, leaves, fruits, buds and roots, using their trunks. Elephants use their trunks to drink as well as feed, by sucking up water and then spraying it into their mouths.

WILD STATS

PREDATORS humans. Tigers may take newborn Asian elephants. Lions, hyenas, wild dogs and crocodiles may prey on young African elephants

LENGTH 5.5-6.6 metres (Asian elephants), 6-7.5 metres (African elephants)

HEIGHT 2.4-2.9 metres (Asian elephants), 2.2-3.7 metres (African elephants)

WEIGHT 4.7 tons (Asian elephants), 7.5 tons (African elephants)

LIFESPAN 40 years (Asian elephants), 50-70 years (African elephants)

CONSERVATION STATUS

Both species are threatened by hunting for their ivory tusks and by habitat destruction. Elephants are legally 'culled' every year in Africa to provide more space for the growing human population and to prevent excessive damage to the land. Ivory trading has been illegal since 1986. However, this does not stop people hunting elephants for their tusks illegally.

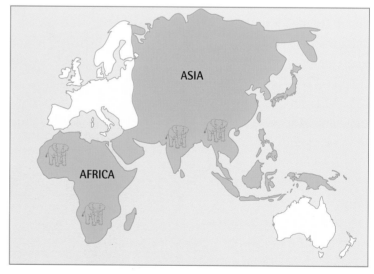

Left, right, left, right ... elephants on parade in a lake's cool waters.

- Aristotle, the Greek philosopher (384-322 BC), was impressed with the great size and intelligence of elephants. It was he who first stated that elephants were scared of mice.

- Elephants have the largest and heaviest brains of all the mammals.

- It is not surprising, then, that elephants understand some human words. This, along with their impressive strength, makes them good working animals. They have been tamed and used as working animals since 5,500 years ago and have even been used to invade countries in wars.

- Elephants have amazing memories, so the saying 'an elephant never forgets' really is true.

- Just like human babies have milk teeth, baby elephants are born with 'milk tusks' (above). These fall out after a year to make way for the adult tusks. But, sadly for elephants, they don't have tooth fairies.

Baby elephants use their mouth to drink their mother's milk from the nipple.

Social life

African elephants spend their time in **maternal** families. The bulls are usually solitary or form small groups. Asian elephants like to spend their time in larger herds of several maternal families. Female and young elephants of both sexes are **social** animals and form close family ties (using smell to recognise each other). When two elephants meet after being separated they 'purr' or 'growl' as a sign of recognition.

Elephants have a great sense of humour. The elephants at Longleat like to sneak up and pinch me with their trunks when I am not looking. If attacked, however, they 'trumpet', raising the trunk in the air and making an incredibly loud sound that can be heard kilometres away. They may also strike their trunks on the ground to show their anger.

Female elephants (cows) give birth to one offspring at a time after a pregnancy that lasts 22 months.

shrewd as a tree shrew

CLASS	Mammalia
ORDER	Scandentia
FAMILY	Tupaiidae
GENUS	6 genera
SPECIES	18 species

These handsome creatures are the romantics of the animal world.

In close up

Tree shrews are only found in Asia, so I have never come across any in my surgery. They are the Asian equivalent of our squirrels and even look like squirrels with their long, pointed snouts, round ears and bushy tails.

These animals have been a puzzle to scientists because they look like shrews (which are **insectivores**) but they also have some primate features. Look at the picture on the right. Do you think they are more like the other **insectivores** or primates in this book?

As you can see from the pictures, they have pointed claws to help grip trees and long tails to help them balance high above the forest floor.

I like these animals because they are the romantics of the mammal world. On first meeting the male and female will sniff each other, mark the other with their own scent and lick or 'kiss' each other all over. They do this daily for up to an hour at a time before setting up family together.

So you could say tree shrews fall in love at first smell!

Habitat

Tree shrews can be both **arboreal** and **terrestrial**. They can be found in the tropical

5 FASCINATING FACTS

- The first reports of the existence of tree shrews come from the explorer Captain James Cook's physician in 1780. Because of the resemblance to a shrew it was then named the tree shrew and this name has stuck, even though it is not true.

- They take great care to wash their faces daily using their paws. Keeping clean and smelling right is incredibly important when you have a daily 'sniffing and scent-marking' ritual.

- Tree shrews are very successful breeders and produce more young than there is room for in the forests they live in.

- Young tree shrews are good at keeping themselves warm without any help from their mother. There is so much fat in the mother's milk that the young can use this to maintain a warm body temperature.

- In the first four weeks of their life tree shrews spend a total of only 90 minutes suckling from the mother and grow to be ten times their original size. That is just three minutes with the mother each day.

With their bushy tails tree shrews look very similar to squirrels.

rainforests of Asia, from India in the west to the Philippines in the east and from South China in the north to Sumatra in the south. Most species, however, live on the island of Borneo.

Diet

Because tree shrews eat insects, worms, invertebrates, fruit and vegetables they are called **omnivores**.

Social life

Being active during the day and resting mainly at night makes tree shrews **diurnal**. They live as pairs in defended territories and raise their young together. To mark boundaries they use secretions from neck glands (hundreds of times each day) or urinate

Despite being called tree shrews, some tree shrews are terrestrial and live on the ground in nests of leaves and twigs. What's in a name?

CONSERVATION STATUS

No threats to these animals at present, but with continued deforestation it is likely these cute animals will come under threat of extinction some time in the not too distant future.

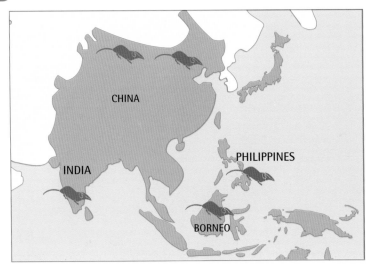

at certain locations at the edge of the territory.

So **territorial** are these small animals that they fight violently over a territory, biting and scratching each other. The loser must move away from the site and find another, uninhabited area to mark as its own territory. If it cannot do this it will die from the stress of being homeless.

A couple of months after first mating with a male the female gives birth to one to four young. Before giving birth the female makes a large nest of leaves in a safe tree hollow. The young are born naked and helpless. Immediately after birth the young drink as much milk from the mother as they can fit in their bellies – until their tummies bulge out as far as they will go. The mother marks the nest with scents that repel males and predators and helps keep the young safe. The male guards the territory while the female suckles the young. Being in a happy relationship makes the animals more relaxed, less stressed and better able to rear their young successfully.

WILD STATS

PREDATORS	not known
LENGTH	13–21 cm
WEIGHT	50–200 g
LIFESPAN	9–10 years

Despite their friendly appearance, tree shrews can fight violently over territory.

elephant shrews: it's just not shrew

CLASS ▸ Mammalia

ORDER ▸ Macroscelidea

FAMILY ▸ Macroscelididae

GENUS ▸ *Rhynchocyon*

SPECIES ▸ *chrysopygus* (golden-rumped elephant shrew)

Neither shrews nor elephants, elephant shrews are distant relatives of dinosaurs!

In close up

Imagine a shrew the size of a cat. Not only are they large but elephant shrews are living dinosaurs (they are close relatives of giants that roamed the earth 30 million years ago). Despite their name, elephant shrews are neither shrews nor elephants. They were mistaken for 'shrews' when first discovered and were named 'elephant' after their long trunk-like snout.

Being **terrestrial** animals,

AFRICA

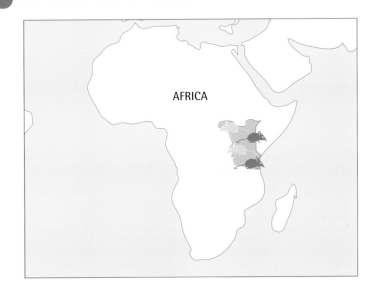

AFRICA

Elephant shrews are threatened with extinction due to spreading population and its effect in reducing numbers of their insect **prey**.

they forage for insects on the ground using their long flexible noses. Large eyes, large ears, a long protruding tongue, long powerful legs and a long, rat-like tail all make elephant shrews odd-looking animals. They also have a greyish brown to reddish coat, forepaws specialised for digging and a coloured spot on the **rump**.

WILD STATS

PREDATORS	black mambas, snake eagles, humans
HEIGHT	27–29.5 cm
WEIGHT	540 g
LIFESPAN	4 years

Habitat

The golden-rumped elephant shrew lives in south-east Kenya. Other species live on **savannahs**, grassland and in

A long nose, large eyes, big ears and a rat-like tail make elephant shrews odd-looking animals don't they?

rocky terrain. Forest elephant shrews use their front paws to scrape together dry leaves to form a nest on the forest floor while others rest in safe places among rocks.

Diet

Elephant shrews are **insectivores**. They sniff out **prey** using their long sensitive noses, but also have good eyesight to spot moving insects, and large ears to hear insects or **predators** with.

Social life

Elephant shrews are **social** and live in pairs. They are **diurnal** and **territorial**: each individual defends the territory against members of the same sex (i.e. males chase off other males and females chase off other females). Like any other animal that defends a **territory** elephant shrews spray the boundaries of the range from special **scent glands** in the **rump**. I only have to pick up an elephant shrew and I can smell its strong odour – pooey! Despite sharing a territory the pair hunt alone and sleep in separate nests.

*Elephant shrews sniff out **prey** with their noses, but also have sharp eyes.*

FASCINATING FACTS

- Because of the long hind legs and their ability to jump around quickly elephant shrews are also known as 'rock jumpers'.

- *Macroscelides* means 'large thighs' and *Chrysopygus* means 'golden-rumped' in Greek.

- Elephant shrews do not sleep curled up like other small mammals. Instead, they lay stretched out with the head resting on their front paws, a position you may have seen dogs sleeping in.

- Male elephant shrews have a coloured spot on their rump. The skin under this spot is three times thicker than anywhere else on the body – and there is a good reason for this. An elephant shrew who turns his back on an attacker is likely to get his bottom bitten – right on the coloured spot. Because elephant shrews have such sharp canines they need a bit of protection!

- Even though it is a fraction of the size of a human it can run as fast as you or I can along an open stretch of ground – not bad for such short legs!

Despite their size, elephant shrews can run as fast as you or me! Although I'm not that fast, I expect you are.

the slowest sloth

CLASS	Mammalia				
ORDER	Xenarthra				
FAMILY		Bradypodidae (three-toed)		Choloepidae (two-toed)	
GENUS	2 genera:	*Bradypus*		*Choloepus*	
SPECIES	5 species:	*tridactylus*	*variegatus* *torquatus*	*didactylus*	*hoffmanni*

In close up

Despite looking unlike any other creature on Earth the sloth is actually closely related to the armadillo. But you will not be able to see the similarities because they are all on the inside. When I am operating on animals in the surgery I get an 'inside' view. Of course, you can't do this at home so you will just have to take my word for it!

Sloths have solid bodies, rough silvery-brown hair, a small round head with a flat round face, small ears, long, slender limbs, and sharp claws.

These slow-motion acrobats hang in the trees by their curved claws. They move so slowly through the forest they look like they are sleepwalking. To avoid **predators** sloths stay

A male sloth employs his climbing skills to stay high up in the trees to avoid any predators.

A female three-toed sloth sleeps hanging onto a branch in a rainforest in Central America.

high in the branches. They are well-**camouflaged** from large birds of **prey** and their stillness also makes them hard to spot. However, they are expert climbers and will move very fast through the trees if ever they are attacked.

Because they spend their lives hanging upside down by all-fours their fur grows 'backwards'. This means rain runs off their bellies easily in bad weather.

Habitat

These **arboreal** acrobats, who live in Central and South America's rainforests, spend almost their entire lives in the trees. And one of the mysteries of sloths is how they came to be such good swimmers. But, occasionally, when they have to cross a river and they cannot do so in the trees, they come down and swim like fishes across to the other side.

WILD STATS

PREDATORS	large birds of **prey**, predatory cats, snakes, humans
LENGTH	45–85 cm
WEIGHT	2.3–8 kg
LIFESPAN	up to 40 years

placentals x-posed

Diet

Sloths are **herbivores**. They eat leaves, buds and fruits and, like koalas, never drink because they get all the water they need from their food.

Social life

Sloths are **solitary** creatures and can be both **diurnal** and **nocturnal**. Female sloths give birth to one young at a time and the infant clings onto its mother's fur as she moves through the forest. As with many mammals the male plays no part in bringing up the young.

Sloths are herbivores and live on leaves, buds and fruits which they find in abundance in South American rainforests.

CONSERVATION STATUS

Some species are abundant while others are seriously threatened with extinction. This is due mainly to destruction of their habitat.

SOUTH AMERICA

Sloths are so comfortable hanging upside down that they spend 15 hours a day sleeping in this position and their grip is so strong they never fall. In fact, sloths are the most upside down mammals in the world – they sleep, eat, mate and travel upside down! Because they are such peace-loving animals sloths are easy to tame.

⑤ FASCINATING FACTS

- Sloths are the slowest mammals in the world.

- A sloth's fur often looks greenish. This is thanks to algae that grows on their hair.

- Some sloths spend up to 80 per cent of their lives asleep.

- Sloths spend more time upside down than any other mammal – including bats.

- Sloths only come down to the ground once a week – to go to the toilet! I don't think I would want to wait so long.

Female sloths give birth to one young at a time. The infant will travel around clinging to its mother's fur for at least the first six months of its life.

the friendliest werewolf

CLASS	Mammalia
ORDER	Carnivora
FAMILY	Canidae
GENUS	14 Genera including *Canis*
SPECIES	30 species including *lupus*

In close up

Wolves are members of the dog family. Just take a look at all the different breeds of dog in the world. Every dog, from the Chihuahua to the Great Dane, originated from wolves that were tamed by humans thousands of years ago.

When I started working as a vet at Longleat one of the first cases I had to treat was a wolf named Werewolf. Poor Werewolf needed to have an eye removed. After the operation we became great friends; he was just like a big shaggy sheepdog.

Wolves and dogs have an amazing sense of smell. This is why blind dogs (or wolves with one eye) cope so well – they can interpret smell far better than we can. Just like footballers, wolves tend to get bad knee injuries because they, too, jump around a lot. A lot of the wolf injuries I

This is Werewolf who lives at Longleat. We became great friends, despite the fact that I had to remove one of his eyes.

deal with at Longleat are knee strains from their active lifestyle – I don't know where they get all their energy from!

Habitat

Wolves are very adaptable when it comes to where they live. They can be found in cold Arctic snows, forests and plains, deserts, swamps and the mountains of Alaska, Canada, North America and Western Europe. There are even a few isolated packs living further south, in Arabia and Asia.

In Norway, where I come from, wild wolves live alongside humans. Sometimes they eat sheep and this makes them unpopular with the local farmers. There is a big campaign in Scandinavia to remove them, but I am sure that if more people realised how closely related wolves are to domestic dogs they would feel differently.

Diet

Look at a dog's teeth, they are exactly the same as wolves' teeth. Like all **carnivores**, wolves have large sharp canines which are essential for killing and eating **prey**. Generally they feed on medium-sized mammals like beavers, other dogs and livestock, whose meat is rather tough.

Social life

Wolves are **social** and **diurnal** hunters. Wolf packs are close-knit, small (five to eight members) and have very strict ranks. A wolf earns its place in the pack by fighting with others and the strongest gains the most respect. Because rank is so important for wolves we have to be careful at Longleat to make sure we never remove one from the pack for long. If we did this the wolf may be rejected, or even killed on its return!

Wolves are one of the most **monogamous** mammals in the world. The male and female stay together after mating and both help rear the puppies. In fact, they are so group-

Wolves are dedicated carnivores. Although they are social animals, they tend to hunt alone.

think they circle round and round before going to bed? In the wild, wolves circle round to make a little nest to sleep in. Why do some dogs howl when their owners sing or

oriented that if a parent dies then the rest of the pack will help rear the puppies.

The pack instinct lives on in domestic dogs. So, if you really want to understand your dog you must learn to think like a wolf! Look at the ways pet dogs behave. Why do you

WILD STATS

PREDATORS	humans
LENGTH	100–160 cm wolves
WEIGHT	15 kg (Arabian wolves), 80 kg (grey wolves)
LIFESPAN	10 years (wolves); up to 20 years (domestic dogs)

Wolves have sharp canine teeth – all the better to gobble up their meaty diet.

- There are over 300 breeds of dog. That means humans have 'created' 300 different types of dog from wolf ancestors.

- Because most breeds of dog can mate with each other they all belong to the same species. The puppies of these cross-matings are known as mongrels. Look at a mongrel and see if you can guess which breeds its parents are.

- Mongrels can have very funny names. If you cross a poodle with a jackal you get a pooja and if you cross a poodle with a wolf you get a poowo!

- Wolves have been respected by man throughout history. The Roman author, Pliny the Elder, noted that Germanic tribes would tie female dogs (bitches) to trees in the woods so they would mate with wolves and the puppies would grow up as good hunters.

- Bitches are known to adopt stray young. They have even been known to adopt the orphan young of lions, tigers and a host of other wild animals from zoos!

there is music on the television? In the wild, wolves howl in groups as a way of communicating and bonding with each other as well as advertising their territory to other packs. Why do dogs always sniff each other's bottoms when they first meet? Dogs and wolves can tell a lot about each other from the smell of the **anal glands**. Body language is another important means of communication. Dogs that have had their tails chopped off (docked) have lost an essential tool and are, quite literally, disabled.

If you have a pet dog you must remember it is more

A wolf pack is small but close-knit, each animal earning its place by fighting.

like a wolf than a human. Many people think of their pets as little humans, but this is not good for them. You should always treat a dog like a dog and let him know that you are the head of the pack. Otherwise your dog will misbehave. A happy dog is one that knows how its owner wants it to behave, with lots of space to run around in since they are such active animals.

CONSERVATION STATUS

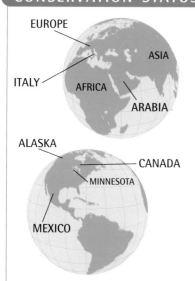

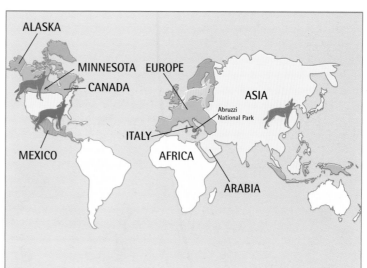

Wolves have been killed by humans for hundreds of years and have been made locally extinct in many countries, like Japan. There are still a few very small, isolated populations in Mexico, Minnesota in the USA and in Italy (Abruzzi National Park).

hare-raising adventures

CLASS	Mammalia
ORDER	Lagomorpha
FAMILY	Leporidae
GENUS	110 genera, including: *Lepus* *Lepus* *Oryctolagos*
SPECIES	44 species, including: *timidus* *europaeus* *cuniculus*
	(Arctic hare) (European/brown hare) (European rabbit)

In close up

Do you have a pet rabbit? Do you know how to tell the difference between a rabbit and a hare? Look closely at the pictures on these two pages and see if you can spot the differences: for instance, hares have longer ears with a black tip at the end (these are known as 'spoons') while rabbit ears are shorter and lacking the black tip.

Some differences are less obvious. Hares run fast and for long distances to escape **predators**, while rabbits dive

Hares use speed to get away from danger...

into their burrows. Young hares are born above ground with a thick coat, eyes open and ready to run from danger. Young rabbits are born in a den and have no hair and their eyes are closed, so they need protection from predators.

Most rabbits and hares are brownish-red in colour, but some, like the Arctic hare, are masters of camouflage and change colour with their surroundings. In the summer these hares are a reddy-brown colour, but in the winter they turn white to blend in with the snow.

The especially large feet of the Arctic hare allow it to jump and run through the snow more easily than you or I can. When I went to Greenland to see the hares I had to put on special snowshoes so I didn't sink into the snow, so I think of these furry friends as the littlest big-feet! It is really exciting watching Arctic hares escape from danger. When I got close the hares saw me as a threat and to get away they all started jumping up and down – it was just like standing in a field of jumping snowballs!

I see a lot of rabbits in my surgery because they make such popular pets. But some-

...while rabbits dive into their burrows when threatened.

times I see wild rabbits which have been brought in suffering from myxomatosis. This is a nasty virus which causes the eyes to fill up with goo until they look like they will pop out, and it turns the poor animal blind. The main problem with this disease is that it can spread from wild animals to domestic pets through fleas, so it is important to make sure the two do not mix with each other and that you have your pet rabbit vaccinated every six months after it is three months old.

Wild rabbits drum on the ground with their hind feet when they are angry. Domestic rabbits also drum on the ground in this way when they are stressed – usually when they have been sitting in a box in my surgery. This explains why most rabbits are called 'Thumper'. However, rabbits are not naturally bad-tempered, so if your pet rabbit thumps a lot this is a sign it is not happy.

Habitat

Hares and rabbits can be found in almost every country and habitat around the world – from the snow-covered Arctic, to the mountainous tropical rainforests of Asia, to the swamps of North America. Because they live on the ground and in burrows they are **terrestrial**. The behaviour of different species is determined by the habitat they live in. For instance, as its name suggests, the Arctic hare lives in the Arctic regions of Greenland and Canada. Arctic hares build castles in the snow to hide in safety during the day, when most of their predators are active. Because the daylight hours are so dangerous, these hares have become **nocturnal**.

Baby hares are called 'leverets' and are brought up only by their mums.

Diet

All hares and rabbits are **herbivores**. They feed on grasses, buds, bark and branches and all have 'double digestion'. This is why you will see your rabbit eating its droppings, so it can absorb some more of the food that has passed through it.

Social life

There is a great deal of variation in the social behaviour of the many different rabbit and hare species. Some are **solitary**, while others, like the Arctic hare, are **social** and spend most of their time in groups of up to several hundred animals. Rabbits and hares may be either **diurnal** or **nocturnal**, depending on the environment in which they live and the predators they must avoid.

'Mad' March hares boxing for female favours.

- Hares sometimes use their large back feet to drum on the ground. This isn't to make music but to send messages to each other – such as warnings of danger.

- Unlike the other **herbivorous** hares, the Arctic hare has been known to take meat from poachers' traps – a risky way to find your food.

- Male hares box with each other over females. They do this in the spring, in March, and this is where the saying 'Mad as a March hare' comes from.

- The largest hares and rabbits can weigh as much as 5 kg – that is larger than some cats.

- Hares can run at speeds of up to 80 kph!

Rabbits are born bald and with their eyes closed. A warm, secure den is needed for their first few days of life.

WILD STATS

PREDATORS	foxes, large birds of **prey**, humans
LENGTH	48–69 cm
WEIGHT	3–5 kg
LIFESPAN	8–9 years

CONSERVATION STATUS

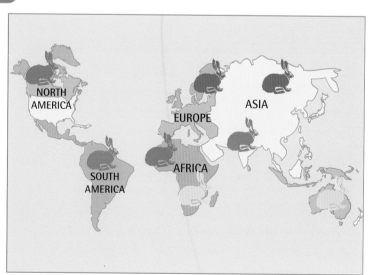

Endangered species of hare and rabbit are at risk from loss of habitat and from poachers who value their soft fur.

caring for your pet rabbit

This is me with my friend Bugsy from Longleat. He loves to run around when he's given a chance and it's very good for him, too.

By looking at how wild rabbits behave we can learn a lot about the best way to keep rabbits in captivity, and here are just a few hints to help you. Think about how rabbits behave in the wild and see if you can come up with any more.

- If you scare a wild rabbit you will see it shoot down the nearest burrow it finds. Rabbit warrens can be enormous since rabbits are born to burrow. So, if you do let your rabbit run free in the garden make sure it doesn't burrow its way under the garden fence. Remember, rabbits are drawn by their stomachs and can easily be enticed back to the cage with some food!

- Wild rabbits live in large family groups, with several animals to keep each other company (preferably from the same litter). Make sure you have females or that any males are **neutered,** otherwise you will end up with more rabbits than you imagined!

- Just like their wild cousins, rabbits love to run and jump about in the open, so why not let your rabbit run about a sealed area of your garden, or even around your living room (rabbits can be litter-trained just like cats). Rabbits that are kept in cramped hutches become stressed, unhappy and difficult to handle.

- Rabbits' teeth grow continuously throughout their lives. Overgrown teeth is one of the most common problems I see in the rabbits brought into my surgery. So let your rabbit chew on lots of different plants, and even sticks and twigs. Other teeth problems are caused by a lack of calcium in the diet. Again, the best way to make sure this doesn't happen to your pet is to give it a varied diet.

mystery mammal

CLASS	Mammalia
ORDER	Hominoidea
FAMILY	Nominidae
GENUS	*Homo*
SPECIES	*sapiens*

In close up

This mammal has a large brain, hair only on its head, armpits and groin, walks on two legs, can talk and uses its hands to make tools. I meet them every day in my surgery and they come in all shapes and sizes. They are **terrestrial** and **diurnal** and care for other animals as well as their own kind; this is most unusual.

They give birth to just one young at a time, although some mothers have two babies (twins) or three babies (triplets) and in very rare cases as many as ten (decaplets)!

Habitat

The mystery mammal can be found all over the world – from the Arctic to the equator. They make their own dwellings which last for many years. Although it does not have fur on its body this mammal can make clothes to keep warm with and is the only mammal capable of making fire.

Diet

This mammal is **omnivorous**. It can grow food and even combine ingredients together to create new foods.

Social life

This is the most **social** of all the mammals. This mammal lives in family groups and the male usually stays with the female to rear children in a **monogamous** relationship. Family groups live together in villages, towns and cities and the children are taught in schools.

WILD STATS

PREDATORS this mammal has few predators. Lions and sharks have been known to kill and eat them, but the biggest killers are tiny organisms which you cannot see without a **microscope**. Viruses and bacteria cause more deaths in this mammal than any large predator

HEIGHT 163–172 cm (males), 147–156 cm (females)

WEIGHT 75 kg (males), 52 kg (females)

LIFESPAN 69 years (men), 76 years (women)
This varies between countries, depending on the medicines available

the mystery mammals are revealed...

You have probably guessed by now that

WE

are the mystery mammals!

Humans have the ability to save all other animal **species** from danger. But all too often we cause them harm instead. Some people kill animals for sport or money. Some of us train as vets to treat sick and injured animals in the hope that we can make their lives better in some way. I hope this book has given you more of an idea about the world of mammals: the different forms and behaviours, and the influences we have had on them, and sometimes them on us.

⑤ FASCINATING FACTS

Humans get up to some pretty strange things and here are just a few;

• Modern humans have been around for about 100,000 years. That may sound a long time to you and I, but compared to many other mammals we haven't been around for very long at all.

• The first humans came from Africa and spread out to all four corners of the globe. As we moved into new countries we altered the landscape and the way the local animals lived.

• The tallest man ever was 272 cm tall and the tallest woman ever was 247 cm. Get a friend to measure you and look at the difference.

• The heaviest man ever weighed more than 635 kg (that's over 100 stone) – it took 13 people just to roll him over in his bed.

• The greatest number of children born by one woman was 55. Imagine trying to remember the names of 54 brothers and sisters.

glossary

ABORIGINE   An **Aborigine** is a native person of Australia.

ALPHA-MALE   The **alpha-male** is the dominant male in a group of chimpanzees.

AMPHIBIAN   **Amphibians** are animals that live on land and in damp places, but must return to the water to breed. Examples of **amphibians** include frogs and salamanders.

AMPHIBIOUS   An **amphibious** mammal is one that lives both on land and in the water, like the duck-billed platypus.

AQUATIC   An **aquatic** animal is one that lives in water, for example sea cows are aquatic.

ARBOREAL   Animals that live in trees are **arboreal**, for example. most monkeys are **arboreal**.

BALEEN PLATES   Plates around a whale's mouth made of bone and fringed with bristles, which strain plankton from water.

BIPEDAL   Mammals that walk on two legs or feet are called **bipedal** – 'bi' = 'two', 'pedal' = 'feet'

CAMOUFLAGE   An animal is **camouflaged** when its body colours and patterns blend in with its surroundings. This is especially important for animals that are hunted by others.

CARNIVORE   A **carnivore** is an animal that eats meat. Most carnivores are hunters, but some eat animals that have already been killed and abandoned.

CASTRATE   This is an operation that vets perform on male animals' **genitals** to prevent them from making females pregnant.

CLASS   Animals are placed into groups according to who they are most closely related to. All the **mammals** form the class mammalia because they share the same basic characteristics.

CLOACA   The **cloaca** is the hole in **monotremes** and **marsupials** through which waste (droppings and urine) is passed. Young are also born through this hole. Humans and other placental mammals do not have a cloaca – we have two (males) or three (females) separate holes.

DEHYDRATE   Animals **dehydrate** when they do not drink enough water. When you are **dehydrated** you feel dizzy and sick.

DIET   The **diet** of a mammal is what it eats, for example the diet of koalas is eucalyptus leaves.

DINGO   Wild dog that lives in Australia and is also a **mammal**.

DIURNAL   A **diurnal** animal is one which is most active during the day (like you).

ECHO-LOCATION   **Echo-location** is the way bats find food. The bat makes high-pitched squeaks and listens out for the echoes. These echoes tell the bat where the **prey** is.

FAMILY   A group of animals from the same **order** that are more closely related to each other than any other animals in the same **order** (e.g. there are 36 **families** of rodents within the **order** rodentia).

FRUGIVORE   A **frugivore** is an animal which eats fruit.

GENITALS   The sexual organs of an animal.

GENUS   A group of animals from the same **family** that are more closely related to each other than any other animals in the same **family** (e.g. there are 400 **genera** of rodents, including Mesocricetus).

GLAND   A special type of cell that produces a specific substance (e.g. sweat glands produce sweat).

HABITAT   The **habitat** of a mammal is the kind of place it lives in (e.g. the rainforest is the habitat of flying lemurs).

HAREM   A **harem** is a group of females who live together with one male.

HERBIVORE   A **herbivore** is an animal which eats plants.

HIBERNATE   Animals that **hibernate** spend the cold winter months asleep (like hedgehogs).

LIMB	A **limb** is an arm or leg.
LIONESS	A **lioness** is a female lion.
MAMMARY GLANDS	Milk secreting organs of female mammals with which they nurse their young.
MATERNAL	**Maternal** relates to the mother. A **maternal** family means the mother and her babies.
MICROSCOPE	A **microscope** is a piece of equipment you use to look at very small objects.
MONOGAMOUS	A **monogamous** couple is a pair of animals that mate only with each other and the father helps raise the offspring.
NEUTER	An operation performed by vets on female animals that prevents them becoming pregnant.
NOCTURNAL	A **nocturnal** animal is one which is active during the night.
OMNIVORE	An **omnivore** is an animal that eats both plants and meat.
ORDER	An **order** is a group of animals that are closely related (all the rodents, for example, are more closely related to each other than to mammals from any other **order**). There are 20 **orders** within the **class** of mammals, all of which are featured in this book.
PLAIN	A large, flat area of land.
POD	A **pod** is the name given to a group of whales.
PREDATOR	A **predator** is an animal that hunts other animals (e.g. the lion is the predator of the African elephant).
PREY	**Prey** animals are hunted by **predators** (e.g. bats **prey** on insects, and bats are the **prey** of some **nocturnal** birds).
PRIDE	A **pride** is the name given to a group of lions.
REGURGITATE	When an animal **regurgitates** food it vomits the food from the stomach to the mouth, where it can further break it down by chewing before swallowing it again.
REPTILE	**Reptiles** are cold-blooded animals with an outer covering of scales or plates (e.g. crocodiles, lizards and snakes). They lay eggs or the young develop in eggs retained inside the mother.
RUMP	The **rump** is the backside of an animal.
SAVANNAH	Open grasslands that cover much of Africa.
SCENT GLANDS	**Scent glands** are glands on an animal's skin that produce smell.
SCENT MARK	Animals **scent mark** an object when they rub **scent** from their **scent glands** onto it. They may do this to pass information to other animals or mark the boundaries of their **territory**.
SEDATE	Vets often **sedate** dangerous animal before they can get near them. This is often done with a dart, and puts the animal into a deep sleep.
SOCIAL	A **social** animal is one that spends a lot of time with other animals.
SOLITARY	A **solitary** animal is one that spends a lot of time alone.
SPECIES	Animals that can mate with one another are the same **species**. So, the golden hamster is one **species** of rodent while the guinea-pig is another.
STEPPE	Grassy, treeless plain.
TERMITES	**Termites** look like ants with wings.
TERRESTRIAL	A **terrestrial** animal is one which spends most of its time on or under the ground.
TERRITORIAL	A **territorial** animal is one which guards the area of land where it lives against trespassers.
TERRITORY	A **territory** is the area an animal lives in and guards against trespassers.